a context for
CHRISTIANITY
in the
21ST
CENTURY

a context for
CHRISTIANITY
in the
21ST
CENTURY

JOANMARIE SMITH

ThomasMore
A DIVISION OF TABOR PUBLISHING
Allen, Texas

Send all inquiries to:
Thomas More Publishing
200 East Bethany Drive
Allen, Texas 75002–3804

Printed in the United States of America

ISBN 0–88347–292–9

1 2 3 4 5   99 98 97 96 95

In loving memory of

Jean M. Roulet

ACKNOWLEDGMENTS

❋

Work began on the topics of this book during a year-long sabbatical given to me by colleagues and the administration of The Methodist Theological School in Ohio. The year was spent at the Institute for Ecumenical and Cultural Research at Collegeville in Minnesota. The Director, Patrick Henry, and Associate Director, Dolores Schuh, were unstinting in their support and practical suggestions during my time there. But I must also acknowledge those friends who have always supported my work, and this book was no exception: my sister Suzanne Smith, Maria Harris, Regina Coll, Gloria Durka, Elaine Roulet and her sister Jean who took such delight in its progress and to whom this book is dedicated. Her untimely death is still a source of great sorrow. Finally, I want to acknowledge the new energy and insights I have received as a gift from recently made friends in Mexico, especially Maria del Socorro Fragoso Nevarez.

❋

"Evangelizing from the Perspective of Beauty," and "Teaching Toward Conversion": Reprinted from the journal, *Religious Education*, Volume 87, 88 (respectively), Number 4, by permission from the publisher, The Religious Education Association, 409 Prospect Street, New Haven, CT 06511–2177. Membership information available upon request.

"Conversion: A Natural Phenomenon," reprinted from *Journal of Spiritual Formation*, (Dusquesne University, Pittsburgh, PA 15282).

"Ecumenism, Commitment and Evangelism," reprinted from *Quarterly Review*, Volume 9, Number 1 (Spring, 1989), The United Methodist Publishing House, Box 801, Nashville, TN 37202.

CONTENTS

❁

PROLOGUE   9

INTRODUCTION   13

CHAPTER ONE   29
   Shifting Toward Pluralism

CHAPTER TWO   57
   Beyond Relativism

CHAPTER THREE   87
   Conversion

CHAPTER FOUR   111
   Precipitating Conversion

CHAPTER FIVE   135
   Commitment

EPILOGUE   167

ENDNOTES   169

INDEX   183

PROLOGUE

❄

John doesn't answer the doorbell. He suspects that the biblical literalists down the block are ringing it. Not that he minds the interruption of his football game (he prefers the professionals on Sunday), although that certainly enters into his decision. If he's honest with himself, however, the admiration and envy their visits provoke are what make him hide out. And the guilt.

They are so sure of what they believe. So passionate in their believing. They seem physically unable to resist trying to persuade him into their certitude and passionate believing. He is not attracted to their beliefs, but he is envious and admiring of their conviction. And he feels guilty. Why doesn't he believe what he believes with a similarly consuming energy? Why isn't sharing his beliefs a top priority in his life? Did he ever believe that way? Whatever conviction he might have had seems to have leaked away through the years. When had the leakage begun?

Was it the first Bible Study he attended in which the facilitators used the historical critical method? All he seemed to learn was what he did not know—and what was unknown. The apostles did not write the gospels, and we're not sure who did. Paul did not write all the Pauline epistles, and we don't know who did. Moreover, we do not think that Jesus said everything that he is reported to have said in the Scriptures.[1] He had found the study persuasive and fascinating. But it certainly did not promote certainty in one's beliefs. And if you were not certain about what you believed, how could you be passionate in your believing?

His participation in the ecumenical movement had done nothing to plug the leak either, he reflected. He had been instrumental in getting persons from other denominations to preach in his parish pulpit on a regular, if infrequent, basis. Joint prayer services had become *de rigueur* for a while. They had even had a Buddhist and a Hindu give separate courses on their traditions in the adult education program. They had been well attended. Too bad they had not had a Muslim though. Appreciation of that tradition is an absolute necessity these days. The last thought distracts him for a moment. As does the end of the half signaled on TV. But he returns again to the possible connection between his involvement in the ecumenical movement and his flagging faith. He's sure that a connection exists. After a while, the different Christian traditions had not seemed that different. The distinctions became more and more blurred. The openness to other religions further complicated his confusion.

Perhaps more than the doorbell triggered these reflections. Perhaps the bell only surfaced questions suppressed during last week's collection for missionaries in India. Hadn't the church invited a Hindu scholar to give the parishioners a course in her tradition? Implied in the invitation was, "Here is another way to God that we should know about and appreciate." There was even the suggestion that the Hindu way was just as authentic as the Christian way. In fact, John himself had been stunned by the power, beauty, and relevance of that tradition as it was unfolded for him. How was he to reconcile his new appreciation of the Hindu tradition with contributions to missionaries to help convert Hindus from their way? "It was a puzzlement," as the King of Siam might put it.

John worried that he was on the slippery slope to perfunctory Christianity—the faded faith of those who turn to their tradition only to ritualize pivotal life moments. How had the pastor referred to them? "Those we hatch, match, and dispatch." Was the slide inevitable?

No wonder he did not want to answer the doorbell. Or the phone either for that matter. He had no answers; he could not give a reason for the faith that was in him.

*****

John is not atypical. His counterparts are to be found attending many of the mainline Christian churches—or leaving them. The certitudes in which people like John were raised have unraveled and have not been replaced. Some have sought new certainty in fundamentalist denominations. Some have remained in the Church as one might remain in a social club that one has belonged to for years—out of a vague loyalty. Like John, others seek answers if not certainty.

This book is written for these last persons and perhaps even more for those to whom they come seeking a framework within which Christianity can make sense in the context of a secular, pluralistic twenty-first century.

But offering answers is not enough. In an age where the *New York Times* has a special bestseller list devoted to "How To" books, people expect to learn ways to implement the insights they gain. Therefore, the last two chapters of this book suggest practical ways to dispose oneself to conversion and ways to nourish commitment. Conversion to passionate and sustained commitment is a gift, of course, that we cannot command to happen. It is grace. Which is not to say that there is nothing we can do. As Corita Kent remarked about celebration, another sheer gift in life, "If you ice a cake, light sparklers and sing, something celebrative may happen."[2] In other words, there is an asceticism of conversion and commitment, equivalents of icing a cake, lighting candles, and singing, that I outline in this book.

INTRODUCTION

✻

AN APOLOGIA FOR APOLOGETICS

Apologetics is the science of demonstrating the reasonableness of a belief or action to others in terms they can understand. "Always be ready to make your defense to anyone who demands from you an accounting for the hope that is in you; yet do it with gentleness and reverence" (1 Peter 3:15–16). Traditionally, this text acted as the starting gun that moved apologists for faith off their running blocks. But apologetics has fallen on hard times. Perhaps the term itself is the problem.

Apology has come to mean saying, "I am sorry"; it now means *not* offering an explanation, *not* defending oneself. This is just the opposite of its original meaning. Like *flammable* and *inflammable*, which are literally antithetical (the first meaning able to be burned and the second, *not* able to be burned) but are now used interchangeably, so *apology* originally meant mounting a

defense for what was deemed *eminently defensible.*
Compounding the semantic difficulties, our
psychologized culture too often identifies *defense* with
defensiveness and defensive mechanisms. One result of
the pejorative use of *defensive* is the macho injunction:
"Never apologize."

Yet, courses in apologetics were still popular a
generation ago. "The Defense of the Faith" was a popular
topic in publishing too. Most often, however, the author
was defending a particular denominational tradition or
the sponsoring institution rather than the faith. The
advent of the ecumenical movement made such defenses
seem tasteless.[1] Given all these factors, the rehabilitation
of apologetics may be impossible. But its prominent
position in Christian thought through the centuries
suggests its practice can make a significant contribution
to our times.

APOLOGETICS AS CONTEXTUALIZATION

Contextualization was the specifying note of apologetics
in its heyday. Christianity was shown to be both
intelligible and credible to the contemporary mind.
Conversely, elements of the faith were shown to be
compatible, even supportive, of the best elements of the
times and the culture. This compatibility with and
support from his context is what John is looking for. Can
he square his life as a person in the twenty-first century
with a faith that goes back to the first century?

Both the Hebrew and Christian scriptures contain
apologetic elements. That is, throughout the scriptures
the writers attempt to reconcile the religious theses
presented with the thinking of the times. The writers of

the Hebrew Bible repeatedly refer to the history of the Israelites as reason for believing in their chosenness and, therefore, as reason for keeping the covenant. The gospel writers assume this apologetic and attempt to demonstrate that Jesus of Nazareth fulfilled the covenant.

Contextualization continues in the early Church. At Pentecost, Peter addresses the variety of nationalities present in terms of their one cultural constant—familiarity with the Hebrew Scriptures—and locates the novelty he proclaims in that context (Acts 2:16–36). In fact, we can say that the Church is born in a miracle of contextualization.

> Now there were devout Jews from every nation under heaven living in Jerusalem. And at this sound [the wind like Spirit] the crowd gathered and was bewildered, because each one heard the apostles speaking in the native language of each.
>
> *Acts 2:5–6*

Paul's address to the Athenians on their home turf, the symbol of Hellenistic intellectual life and piety, is a paradigm of apologetics as contextualization. First, he recognizes the validity of their religious life. Then, referring to their shrine to an unknown God and quoting a well-known poem, he locates Christianity in a context with which they are familiar.

So Paul, standing in the middle of the Areopagus, said:

> Athenians, I see how extremely religious you are in every way. For as I went through the city and

15

looked carefully at the objects of your worship, I found among them an altar with this inscription, "To an unknown god." What therefore you worship as unknown, this I proclaim to you. The God who made the world and everything in it, the One is Sovereign of heaven and earth, does not live in shrines made by human hands, and is not served by human hands as though God needed anything, since God alone gives to all mortals life and breath and all things. And from one ancestor this God made all the nations to inhabit the whole earth, and allotted the times of their existence and the boundaries of the places where they would live, so they would search for God, in the hope that they would grope for and find this God who is not far from each one of us, for "In this one we live and move and have our being"; as even some of your own poets have said, "For we are indeed the offspring of God."

Acts 17:22–28

The Book of Acts, which records these two scenes, also reports the tensions involved in contextualizing. Luke, the author of Acts, traces the agony of Peter as he attempts to sort out which elements of Christianity are adaptable and which are not (Acts 10). Did the gentile Christians have to be circumcised or keep kosher kitchens? The Council of Jerusalem said "No" and "Partially" (Acts 15). Paul countermands the second decision when he declares that eating meat offered to idols is permissible if this action does not scandalize those who do not know any better (1 Corinthians 8). These brief allusions to contextualizing in early Church history suggest some of the problems involved in the process. Yet, a context is not only necessary to determine meaning; a context is the very condition of existence.

CONTEXT AND MEANING

Dictionaries give us definitions not meanings. What does *bank* mean? Are we talking about the bank of a river or the bank that is a savings institution? A dictionary cannot tell us. We need a context to get the word's meaning. Take the word *couch*. Dictionaries list the genus (a piece of furniture) and species or specifying note (on which persons can sit or lie). But dictionaries also define *couch* as the activity of putting something into words. To learn the meaning, I must know how the word is used in context. The meaning of meaning is the difference something makes.

But the surrounding words are not the only source of context. The inflection, volume, pitch—in sum, the tone with which we articulate a word—conveys meaning, the difference we intend. Facial expressions, gestures, and posture also contribute to the context from which we derive meaning. One can say "Hooray" in a tone or manner that means "Boo." Obviously, therefore, although the notion of context is most often used with regard to the spoken and written word, it has a much broader application.

CONTEXT AND EXISTENCE

As the context of a word can be called its environment, so the environment of any living thing can be called its context. Having made the case that a context is required for a word's meaning, I want to argue that a context is absolutely necessary for any organism's existence. If you plant a watermelon seed in a congenial environment, in the fullness of time you will come upon a fully grown fruit. However, the thick rind, tender red pulp and umpteen pits have not come from the seed. They are the environment organized into a watermelon. The fruit emerges from the environment. The seed "watermeloned" its context. The elements that constituted the soil, water, air, and fertilizer have been reconstituted as watermelon.

The process is duplicated in any living being from amoebas to human fetuses. For the life spark to be fanned into existence and to be sustained, the environment must be incorporated—literally made into the body of the organism. Without such contextualizing, no organism can exist. Fire, although nonliving, provides a vivid image. It lives off its context. Its existence is absolutely dependent upon consuming its "around." Deprived of matter that it can transform into itself, it gasps a few flickers and dies.

CONTEXTUALIZING THE *LIVING* WORD

From its inception, Christianity was conceived as a universal vision, a way of life and a system of beliefs for all peoples and all times. "Go . . . and make disciples of *all* nations . . . teaching them to obey everything that I have commanded you" (Matthew 28:19–20) [Author's italics]. For that teaching to be minimally intelligible to the people of different nations, it had to be in a language they could understand. The apostles could either teach Jesus' language to perspective converts, or they could translate the Good News into the language of the people they were addressing.

From Pentecost on, the Church recognized that God's Word must be in the vernacular. It is a wonderful irony that none of the Gospels were written in Jesus' own Aramaic tongue. Our unfamiliarity with that language probably helped prevent the canonization of any particular language as the repository of revelation—a circumstance almost unique to Christianity.[2]

But translation into the vernacular is the least of the evangelizing task if we believe in the Incarnation—that in Jesus the Word was made flesh. The salvation as well as the scandal in God's Word is its embodiment in a particular time and place, a particular language and culture. Nothing is farther removed from mechanical or philosophical categories than flesh. God's Word-become-flesh is quintessentially organic and concrete. As with any living entity, the Word can only continue to exist where it is nourished by the blood streams of its context. Therefore, the translation to all nations must be of the most comprehensive sort.

Somehow, the life, passion, death, and resurrection of a relatively unknown teacher in the Palestine of two thousand years ago must be translated to our era, our culture, our psyches. The transfer obviously requires translation into a language intelligible to us. But language is not to be confined to the spoken or written word.

Language is a metaphor for a kind of mutual indwelling of psyches, a communication moving towards communion as when one says with some delight, "Now we are speaking the same language."

DIFFICULTIES OF TRANSLATION: TRANSLATING LANGUAGES

Two major difficulties dominate the effort to translate from one language to another. The first is that there is not a word-for-word correspondence between languages. The second is that languages are living entities that can and do change—sometimes quite drastically. The overcoming of both difficulties involves familiarity with the context into which a word is being translated.

Even high-school students of French know enough to translate *comment portez-vous?* as "How are you?" which is what it means, rather than "How do you carry yourself?" which is what it says. The principles of translation tell us to look for dynamic equivalents between languages and cultures. Rather than try to identify formal equivalents (*porter* equals "to carry"), the task is to see how a phrase or symbol or ritual functions in the new context. *Comment portez-vous* functions as a greeting. Therefore, a dynamic equivalent in American English is our typical greeting, "How are you?"

Identity, or at least similarity of response helps us test whether or not we have a functional equivalent. The impact is the same if people react the same. And vice versa. Recently, a Ghanaian priest described how the peoples' reaction to a European priest's Akan version of the *Kyrie Eleison* sent the poor man back to his language dictionary. Instead of "Lord have mercy," he was praying "The Lord is miserable."[3]

Then there are nuances of functional equivalents. It is one thing to know that *Comment portez-vous?* means "How are you?" It is another thing to know when such phrases are properly used. Under what circumstances is the less formal *Ça va* a more appropriate greeting? That insight requires more acquaintance with the French culture of the day and even of the region where you intend to greet people in an intelligible and credible way. Moreover, once words are translated, we have seen that their embodiment in tones and gestures extends the context of meaning. All these insights require a greater familiarity with a culture than that required simply to translate words from one language to another; they require inculturation, the process by which a culture assimilates the faith in terms of its own cultural matrices.[4]

DIFFICULTIES OF TRANSLATION: TRANSLATING BODIES

If inculturation is required for a mere greeting, it stands to reason that translating the living body of Christ requires a radical inculturation. Distinguishing those cultural elements that will nurture the life of the body of Christ, from those that are death-dealing has long been a concern of the Church. But the problem is exacerbated in our day.

For almost a thousand years the worldview of the West distinguished the appearances of things from their reality which "stood under" (substances) those appearances. Appearances were "accidents," that is, they need not be that way. Color, weight, and shape were literally not essential—not the essence of reality. In this context, it was understandable that the essence of the Gospel was thought to be distinct from its cultural expression so that discussions about inculturation revolved around what was essential to the good news and what was merely its packaging.

Whatever was accidental could be adapted, changed, or even abandoned. By definition, not even the Church could tinker with the essence of the faith. These disputes continue, but with a decided disadvantage. There is little agreement these days that the categories of substance and accident are viable. We currently have a more organic view of reality.

An example is as close as my own existence. While some aspects of my self might be more essential to my being, my mind and memory for example as against my hair or heart, all of them are really me. There is no essence of me underlying the appearance of me. My "me" is constitutive of my appearances, and vice versa. My too tallness or too thinness feeds into and out of the development of who I am. Moreover, without a context, I cannot be me. Without the earth to supply nourishment, I cannot even *be*. Without an enveloping culture to supply a vocabulary, I cannot think about myself. I need the words my culture gives me in order to think about anything—including God. Torn from a context, I would be like any vital organ torn from its sources of life; I would die.

But not everything in the environment nourishes my existence. Some elements, like lead for example, poison my embodiedness. Others, like pornography, can poison my imagining power. So while my existence is not sustained from above or from below, but from around—not everything in my "around" is to be absorbed.

Perhaps no people are calling our attention to the role of the "around" more than those in the churches of two-thirds of the world. For example, inculturation or indigenization (contextualization) issues dominate the religious literature from the African Church.[5] Peoples once colonialized by the West are examining the degree to which the faith shared with them included Western ways of thinking and Western customs as well as Western languages. Theologians and especially liturgists are making prodigious efforts to recast God's Word in the context of their own cultures. The focus of these efforts lies in discerning the nourishing streams of their cultures from those that are death-dealing. Is monogamy merely a Western custom baptized by Western Christianity? Can polygamy be similarly baptized? Or is polygamy fundamentally at odds with the Good News? The final answers to these questions are not yet in—at least not from the Africans.

Ironically, similar work is not being done in the West. There is the sense that the Gospel is already contextualized here. But the underpinnings of our culture have radically shifted in this century, and those underpinnings and the insights they have structured have yet to be thoroughly absorbed. Cultural lag is inevitable.[6] Changes in the way we do things usually far outdistance examination of the thought patterns that allow these changes. Einstein once remarked, "Everything has changed but our thinking." As far as religion goes, we seem stuck in the Age of Enlightenment. Two views of religion contribute to our remaining stuck: the view that religion is a private affair and the view that Christianity is essentially countercultural.

RELIGION AS A PRIVATE AFFAIR

The Enlightenment refers to an eclectic system of beliefs popularized by the French *philosophes* of the eighteenth century and canonized in the political revolutions of that era. Those beliefs stressed the power of reason and the irrationality of faith—in particular religious faith. (I treat the view of knowledge bequeathed to us from the Enlightenment in the next chapter.) Henceforth, any "enlightened" state could not support any particular religion. But it could preside over the enlightened tolerance of all religions. The exaltation of the rights of individuals was a central tenet of the Enlightenment, and religion was, after all, an individual choice.

In fact, those nation states that observed tolerance provided a healing oasis from the holy wars and persecutions that had marked our history of intolerance—holy wars and persecutions that persist to this day in intolerant areas.

But toleration of religious beliefs fostered the privatization of religion. As the notion of a state religion fragmented into many unsupported religions, religion left the public domain. For many, religious beliefs took on the character of what you did in your bedroom or what you said to your therapist; they were no one else's business. With privatization, the need to defend one's religious beliefs to the public in an intelligible and credible way also waned.

CHRISTIANITY AS COUNTERCULTURAL

Paradoxically related to the privatization of religion is the argument that religious beliefs are most authentically expressed when and where they sharply oppose the prevailing culture. If the centerpiece of a culture is persecution and prosecution of religious adherents, certainly such adherents are understandably counter-cultural. But is Christianity intrinsically countercultural? John Coulson, the author of *Religion and Imagination*, reminds us: "If anything, history asserts the contrary. When a religious claim ceases to find convincing embodiment or ground in its contemporary culture, it soon degenerates into an implausible rhetoric."[7]

The people who would dispute Coulson cite biblical texts that seem to equate the world (and thence the cultures that construct the world) with all that is evil and to be avoided. Those who maintain, as I do, that Christianity emerges from and is transforming of culture cite such texts as "God so loved the world that he gave his only Son, so that everyone who believes in him may not perish but may have eternal life" (John 3:16).

If Christianity were just a case of texts, we could continue the discussion at this level. Even on this level, we must note that in their writings the first Christians used the science of the times, the political categories of their day, the language of the kitchen table to express their faith. There is not a single significant word in the Christian scriptures that cannot be found in the secular literature of the times.[8] Moreover, if one believes that we are not just talking about translating a word, we are also and more profoundly talking about translating an enfleshed Word, the Body of Christ, then we must look to the Incarnation for the principle of inculturation. Missiologist Robert J. Schreiter describes the principle reward:

> God did not first conform us to his reality in the full revelation of himself to us in Jesus. Rather, Jesus appeared as the revelation of God under the concrete historical circumstances of a people in the Mediterranean basin. None of the cultural rules were suspended to make this revelation possible; yet within the limitations (and possibilities) of that culture the kingdom of God could be announced—and inaugurated— effectively.[9]

The remainder of this book is an essay in contextualizing Christianity for the twenty-first century. I will tease out from the Post-Enlightenment findings of several disciplines a nourishing "around" for the faith. I will address the questions unique to the contemporary inquirer: Can I be a passionately committed follower of Christ without the certainty that this is the only way of salvation? Can I, should I, go into all nations baptizing them in the name of the Trinity? "Yes" is the response that organizes the following chapters.

Chapter One traces the evolution of the current worldview in the West. The centerpiece of any worldview is the way we think that we know reality. In Chapter One, I show that at one time we thought we really knew only what had been revealed. This period was succeeded by the conviction that genuine knowledge was obtained only through experience—a bequest of the

Enlightenment. As we move into the twenty-first century, most thinkers believe that we do *not* know in any of the old senses of "know." Knowledge is something we construct with our imagination, but we must not confuse imagination with fantasy. However, the temptation to relativism in a pluralistic context is obvious.

Chapter Two examines imagination more closely as well as a theory of truth that navigates the shoals between relativism and dogmatism. I argue that, while we cannot know reality in any point-for-point correspondence way, that does not mean that one opinion is as good as another. I offer criteria for judging some opinions about reality as better than others. These criteria are then applied to religion.

Chapter Three describes conversion as the dynamic that heats up our believing and brings it center stage in our lives. I examine different ways in which conversion has been defined. Then I look to some analogies to religious conversion that different authors have proposed. From these analogies I distill a single pattern of conversion. Finally, I explore God's role and our role in the phenomenon.

In Chapter Four, I spin out those elements of the pattern in which our cooperation is most likely to be crowned by conversion—specifically contemplation and conflict. I suggest exercises that invite contemplation and promote the conflict that appears to be central to the moment of conversion.

Chapter Five describes a conversion that has "taken" as transformation—an *ongoing* commitment to the object of our believing, to the centrality of God in our lives. Evangelism is the natural effect of this transformation.

The appropriateness of evangelizing in a pluralist era is examined and proclaimed.

❀

CHAPTER ONE

SHIFTING TOWARD PLURALISM

William James said that landlords would do better to check the worldviews of prospective tenants rather than their credit ratings.[1] Our worldview is likely to indicate whether we will befriend the neighbors and keep the area clean *as well as* pay the rent on time.

Worldviews are embedded in our most innocent exchanges. For example, the simple greeting "Good morning, Joanmarie" is rife with major (and disputable) philosophic positions. To cite just a few:

* Communication is possible, which in turn implies an intelligible universe. (The parents of teenagers as well as professional philosophers might dispute both these positions.)

* There is a variety of kinds of stuff in this universe. (We do not greet tables and chairs.)

* This is, if not the best, at least not the worst of all possible worlds. (Among nonphilosophers, positions on this view can vacillate from day to day, not to say from hour to hour.)

* There is some common understanding of time.

IN THE MATTER OF WORLDVIEWS

We rarely tease out the worldviews in our conversation however. So much the worse for landlords. If one were to construct a rental form that sought to discover the worldview of an applicant, a major section of the document would have to be devoted to the question "How do you think that you know—anything?" The answer to this question forms the cornerstone on which we structure our models of the world and our place in that world.

To date, three dramatically different answers have been given to this question. The shift from one answer to another marks three great watersheds in Western history.[2] The shift turns on what people think of as grounding knowledge or on how we determine that something is true. Classically, knowledge has been defined as *justified, true belief.* How we justify a belief or on what grounds we conclude that an idea or perception is true tells us what knowledge is for us.

In this chapter, I illustrate the three shifts in our foundation of knowing by focusing on moments in each period that contributed to or, at least, certainly manifested the distinctive notion of knowledge in the era.

* The first epoch is marked by the conviction that we know only what has been revealed. Revelation is the ultimate authority for

anything we claim to know. This answer dominates until the middle of the seventeenth century or more precisely until June 22, 1633.

* The second epoch lasts until our own century and is characterized by the insight that we know only what we experience. "Show me," say the Missourians, succinctly capturing the epistemology of this era. "My senses will tell me what is actually the case; what is true."

* In our own time, many of our most revered thinkers believe that we cannot know in the classical sense. What we do is imagine and our most fruitful imaginings are called knowledge. "Truths" seem to be no more than those beliefs about which there is a consensus.

KNOWLEDGE AS REVELATION

Our earliest recorded history is religious history. God or the gods reveal to selected persons all that is needed to live a meaningful life. Lycurgus and Moses are typical of this history. Lycurgus is the leader who, according to legend, received the constitution of the city of Sparta from the gods. Moses, of course, is the one to whom God gave the Law that was to shape the life of the Israelites. To know reality in this era, one must have it revealed to him or her (usually him) or attend to someone to whom it has been revealed.

When Moses' father-in-law asks him why people keep coming to him all day and well into the night, Moses answers, "Because the people come to me to inquire of God. When they have a dispute, they come to me and I decide between one person and another, and I make known to them the statues and instructions of God" (Exodus 18:15–17). Moses' weariness and his father- in-law's prodding persuade him to enlist helpers to dispense the revelations. "Moses chose able men from all Israel and appointed them as heads over the people, as officers over thousands, hundreds, fifties, and tens. And they judged the people at all times; hard cases they brought to Moses, but any minor case they decided themselves" (Exodus 18:25–27).

The Mosaic times (circa 1200 B.C.E.) exemplify an era that must have begun centuries earlier. The Platonic philosophy of Augustine of Hippo (354–430 C.E.) set in relief the rational structure that would undergird the era of revelation as knowledge for more than a thousand years after Augustine's death.

Plato and The Cave

Philosophy began in the sixth century B.C.E. as the attempt to reflect on the nature of reality apart from the speculations of any particular religious perspective. Plato (428–348 B.C.E.) does this with such power and compelling logic that in the twentieth century the great thinker Alfred North Whitehead can still say that all subsequent Western philosophy is simply a footnote to Plato.[3] But Plato has also been described as the outstanding philosopher of the primordial mentality ("the thinker who succeeded in giving philosophic currency and validity to the modes of life and behavior of archaic humanity"),[4] a life and behavior marked by knowledge as revelation.

Plato is convinced that we can have justified true belief, that we can have knowledge and certitude. But not easily. Knowledge cannot be of the particular things we see around us, this Sally Jones or that apple, but only of the formula or *eidos* or universal notion of woman or apple realized temporarily in these individuals. Since to be certain knowledge must be unchanging, we cannot have knowledge as such of Sally Jones or a Granny Smith apple; they will pass out of existence. Knowledge can only be of the unchanging essences that make these things a woman or an apple. In fact, something is real only to the extent that it more or less adequately reflects any particular essence. We hear echoes of Platonic thought in our conversation when we speak, for example, of a *real* friend, that is, someone who approximates an *eidos* or ideal of friend in some exemplary way. (The Greek *eidos* is usually translated as "form" in Plato's works, but the English *idea* and *ideal* come from the Greek and are philosophically related to Plato's use of the term, especially *ideal*.)

In the famous allegory of the cave in Plato's *Republic* (Book VII), he paints a vivid metaphorical picture of the painful journey to knowledge. A man is chained with other men in a cave where they see shadows of art works being carried into the cave. The men mistakenly believe these objects to be real. But they are only imitations of imitations of imitations of reality. The man is unchained to realize that what he and the others have been counting as real are only shadows (the first imitation) of statues, which are likenesses of persons (the second imitation). As he is dragged up into the light of the Sun, the source of all reality, he experiences the world of the *eidos* and simultaneously "knows" that he and the others in the cave are mere imitations of the really real too. He has seen the Sun, the *eidos* of the Good (God?), "the universal cause of all things right and beautiful—the source of truth and reason" (517 b 8–c 4).

When Plato describes the philosopher/king who should rule the Republic, the pre-eminent qualification is that he is one who has made the allegorical journey, who has in Plato's words "true knowledge." Plato had no patience with the democratic form of government. The "demos" are too often like those who remain in the cave, never knowing that they do not know. The philosopher/king, on the other hand, is god-like. When philosopher/kings die, "the city will give them public memorials and sacrifices and honour them, if the Pythian oracle consents, as demi-gods, and at any rate as blessed and divine" (540 a 7–c 2).

What Plato did for those who preceded him, "giving philosophic currency and validity to the modes of life and behavior of archaic humanity," Augustine will do for the generations who succeed him.

Augustine and The City of God

In 422, Saint Augustine (354–430 C.E.) of Hippo in North Africa published the last section of his great work *The City of God*. For fourteen years he had labored to produce this masterpiece. Completed, the book, along with his other writings, would provide the structure upon which Christianity systematized its doctrines, laws, and spirituality for the next millennium.

Along with the Neoplatonist philosophers who lived, thought, and wrote between Plato and Augustine—most particularly Plotinus (205?–270 C.E.)—Augustine locates the forms or *eidos* in God's mind. "The ideas are certain archetypal forms or stable and immutable essences of things, which have not themselves been formed but, existing eternally and without change are contained in the divine intelligence" (*De Ideis*, 2). Then, in *The City of God*, Augustine fixes the locus of revelation. He sees the City of God, the spiritual City of Jerusalem, as embodied within the Church because only the Church embodies true justice. The Church in and through its officials will mediate the *eidos* in God's mind to the faithful.

One scholar, commenting on Augustine's claim that "Christianity is the one true philosophy,"[5] says, "He meant that rational inquiry, illumined by the products of revelation accepted on faith is the only *wisdom*, the only adequate account of things human and divine."[6] In other words, we really know only what has been revealed and the Church is the repository of that revelation. This notion of knowledge will reign unchallenged in the West until the sixteenth century when a competing source of knowledge begins to emerge.

SUBVERTING THE ERA OF REVELATION

As the answer to how we know (it has been revealed) and what we know (the truth), revelation did not quite survive the seventeenth century. Three major events contributed to the subversion of this answer, which had served civilization so well for so many millennia: the discovery of the New World, the breakup of Christendom, and the explosion of science.[7] In this section, I will concentrate on the trauma of incorporating the concept of a New World into a sixteenth-century psyche and the trial of Galileo, which dramatized so vividly the end of one era and the beginning of another.

The New World

Ten years after Columbus's first voyage to "India," Amerigo Vespucci, on a similar trip, concluded that South America was a New World. It is almost impossible for us to imagine the impact of this event on the people of that time. A marvelous little book *The Invention of America* by Edmundo O'Gorman, captures something of the novelty.

O'Gorman describes the notion of one world that prevailed. We tend to use the terms *world* and *universe* interchangeably. But for the ancients, the "universe" comprised everything that existed. The "world" was only that part of "the orb of earth" that was *oikoumene*— home; that part of the island of our planet that was inhabited or inhabitable by humans. The Greek and later the Latin word for *world* is derived from *oikos*, the word for house. *World* therefore referred to the living quarters of human beings as revealed by the Deity.[8]

Some people had speculated that there might be other inhabitable areas of the earth, other worlds, but the dominant view had ruled out this possibility: it was incompatible with the species having been spawned by one couple as revealed in the Bible. Moreover, Augustine had written that the citizens of the City of God will come only from Europe, Asia, and Africa, that is, *the World*.[9]

Commenting on this now thoroughly Christianized version of the revelation-as-reality worldview, O'Gorman writes:

This mystic, geographical conception of the Church Fathers was inherited by later Christian writers, who gave it new support in numerous and varied allegorical interpretations. They saw in the threefold division the geographic symbol of the Holy Trinity; they believed its origin to be the distribution of the earth among Noah's sons; they believed that the three wise men who came to pay homage to the new born Jesus represented the three parts of the world, and they also saw in this division an illustration of certain passages in the Gospel and of the mystic perfection of the number three.[10]

People of the times even saw the Pope's three-tiered miter as a symbol of the threefold division of the world.[11] Given this mindset, how could Columbus have stumbled upon anything other than Eastern Asia? After his third journey, he toyed with the idea that the land he was skirting in his explorations was *orbis alterius*, another island, a fourth part of the earth. O'Gorman reminds us that the idea of a plurality of worlds was an heretical one, unacceptable to Church authority. We might imagine, therefore, that Columbus was somewhat relieved when his fourth journey reconvinced him that he had indeed reached the Indies.

We can understand, too, why the expression "New World" refers not only to a hemisphere, but to a whole new way of looking at reality. A person who has had the experience of a "New World" breaking in upon her or him can appreciate the effect that Amerigo Vespucci's letter, in which he uses the term (the so-called *Mundus*

Novus Letter of 1503), had upon its recipients. Such a person might also have a unique insight into why this fourth part of the earth was named after Amerigo rather than Christopher.

In a subsequent letter (1504) where he describes the land masses in greater detail, Vespucci no longer uses the term *New World*; in fact he does not name these lands at all. O'Gorman offers this explanation: "He must have been fully aware that he had resorted to an inadmissible concept, that of plural worlds, but either he could think of no alternative or he hesitated to assume responsibility for proposing a new concept to express the new geographical picture of the world which he evidently had in his mind."[12]

Cosmographiae Introductio, published in 1507, unleashes forever the trauma of a "fourth part" of the inhabitable universe. The famous map of Waldseemuller, which is the first chart to show the name *America,* is in this publication. Here it is determined that since this world was "conceived" by Amerigo Vespucci it should be called the Land of Amerigo or America (since Europe and Asia bear feminine names.) The difficulty with which this idea was embraced is suggested by the return of Waldseemuller himself to the notion that the newfound land in the Northern Hemisphere was Asia.[13]

Only with the maps of Gerardus Mercator in 1538 is the "Invention of America" and the notion of a "New World" firmly fixed in the psyche of the Old World. By this time, the Reformation, with its attack on papal authority and its emphasis on personal experience, was in full flower. Thus, the idea of a New World became more comprehensible than it could have been in the past. So, the discovery of the New World was just one of the many cracks being introduced into the cornerstone of an era characterized by revelation as the ultimate arbiter of what we know.

Galileo's Trial

In 1543 the first printed copy of Copernicus's *Revolution of the Heavenly Orbs* was delivered to the author, reputedly on his deathbed. Scholars debate whether he had made sure that the text would be published only near the close of his life. In any case, his death was timely in that it delivered him from the arrows and slingshots that Galileo would suffer almost a hundred years later for "proving" Copernicus's thesis that the earth revolves around the sun and not vice versa.

The revolution Copernicus had described was anything but rapid or violent, but the *idea* was so dislocating, literally and figuratively, that the term has passed into our language from his title as a radical and frequently violent change.[14] In Chinese, the term that translates as revolution in English literally means "to change the command of heaven."

At his trial, Galileo offered a two-fold defense. First, he tried to make the case that he had not taken a position in *The Dialogues Concerning the Two Chief World Systems*. What he had presented was a conversation in which only one of the participants was a proponent of the Copernican theory. The second element in his defense revolved around a visit he had made to Rome in 1616. During the visit he had received from Cardinal Bellarmine an affidavit permitting him to take the opinion of Copernicus hypothetically and use it in that manner in his work. We know the outcome of the trial, but sections of the transcript so vividly capture the era I have been describing that I must quote Galileo.

He has just been asked why he went to Rome in 1616. He answers:

> The occasion for which I was in Rome in the year 1616 was that, hearing questions raised about the opinion of Nicholas Copernicus concerning the motion of the earth and stability of the sun and the order of the celestial spheres, in order to assure myself against holding any but holy and Catholic opinions, *I came to hear what must be held concerning this matter.*[15]

Shades of the people beseeching Moses to know what to think and what to do.

Perhaps the most surprising part of Galileo's testimony is the fact that he meant it. Stillman Drake, the foremost Galilean scholar, is convinced that Galileo's first concern was the Church.[16] However, it is not surprising that even after Galileo swore that he adhered to the fixed earth and moveable sun theory as prescribed by "sublime authority," he was sentenced to life imprisonment on June 22, 1633. Six months later the sentence was commuted to house arrest—for life.

Legend has long had it that, after retracting his position, Galileo muttered a defiant, *"Eppur si muove!"* (Yet, it [the earth] still moves.)[17] It hardly matters whether he said this; the earth in fact did keep moving. The authority of Galileo's experience with and through his telescopes won the war if not the battle.

KNOWLEDGE AS EXPERIENCE

My mother was born shortly after the turn of the century. I remember her telling me that when she was twenty-five a physician had encouraged her to have children as soon as possible because she was already middle-aged. She was; fifty was the life expectancy of a woman then. Today it is seventy-eight. Such an extension of life in such a short time has to have the appeal and fascination of the miraculous (*mira*—look!) Tragically, that increased life expectancy does not extend across the continents or even across the racial and class lines of the United States. The tragedy lies in the fact that it so easily could because it is *scientia* (knowledge, science) that has made at least another half life possible to all of us.

Few people will dispute the domination of scientific achievements on the Western imagination. The sciences alone among the disciplines seem to make progress. No one claims that we have learned a great deal more about writing plays since Shakespeare's time (1564–1616), or even more about historiography since the time of Herodotus (485–425? B.C.E.), the Father of History. Rather, reading contemporary critics, we might be inclined to think these other disciplines had peaked years or centuries ago and that it has all been downhill ever since. On the other hand, who among us does not think that a cure for cancer is just around the corner? Or that we can anticipate breakthroughs in science that will be every bit as revolutionary as the Copernican, Darwinian, or the Einsteinian breakthroughs? Many of us might also think that science has not only extended our life span but has also enhanced the quality of that life. No wonder then that science dominates our imagination.

41

From the very beginnings of the scientific revolution in the sixteenth century, the achievements and potentialities of science mesmerized people. How was this explosion of knowledge possible? When one happens to make an especially good cup of coffee, the task becomes that of trying to retrace the method by which this small miracle occurred. Just so, some of the best minds of Europe attempted to distill from the scientific achievements of the day the method that had generated such major miracles as the discovery of a New World, our relocation in the universe, and the inexpensive distribution of this information through the printing press.

Two descriptions of the scientific method vied for prominence in the seventeenth century. Bacon published *Novum Organum* (1616), literally, "The New Tool"; Descartes wrote the *Discourse on Method* (1637). Descartes has gone down in the books as the supreme rationalist because he emphasized the mathematical and deductive method (from the general to the particular). Bacon, on the other hand, emphasized experiment and induction (reasoning from individual facts to a general conclusion).

Bacon's views won the day and even the succeeding centuries, perhaps because some of the great scientific minds of the time subscribed to it.[18] Robert Boyle (1627–1691) and Robert Hooke (1635–1703), both of whom are memorialized by scientific laws that bear their names, were two of these subscribers. Undoubtedly, however, it was the support of Bacon's theories by Newton (1642–1727), perhaps the greatest scientist until Darwin and Einstein, that installed Bacon's theories as *the* scientific method.

Newton's work constituted a revolution in the way we see the world almost as bruising as Galileo's vindication of Copernicus's view. Newton made many lasting contributions to science, but his description of the laws of motion and gravity had the most effect outside of physics. These laws, applicable to every object in the universe, seemed to make of the universe one huge machine ruled by inflexible and *discoverable* rules. If Newton supported the insights of Bacon, Bacon must be correct.

Are not children still learning the scientific method as observe, hypothesize, experiment, and verify? During the eighteenth and nineteenth centuries, the sciences appeared to go from triumph to triumph under this rubric that we obtain knowledge, advance *scientia* by experiment, that is, empirically. Which is to say, justified true belief is acquired through experience. It is not out of the blue that Newton's insights are forever connected to the experience of being hit in the head by an apple.

No longer are ecclesiastical authorities the final arbiter of reality. To get some sense of how radical is the shift from the conviction that we know only what is revealed, to we know only what we experience, consider the reinterpretation of the Jewish and Christian Scriptures in the last century. All but the most ardent biblical literalists among us reinterpret the creation stories of Genesis to incorporate Darwin's evolutionary conclusions derived from his experience of the Galapagos Islands.

Where religious knowledge had shaped previous ages, this new way of obtaining knowledge shaped the following centuries. To be called a "Newtonian" thenceforth meant that you treated things without superstition or so-called religious prejudice. Nothing distinguishes this new era from the previous era as well as the oft-quoted conversation between Napoleon (1769–1821) and the French mathematician and astronomer, Laplace (1749–1827):

> **N.** "M. Laplace, they tell me you have written this large book on the system of the universe, and you have never even mentioned its Creator."

> **L.** "I had no need for that hypothesis."[19]

Having been enlightened about the way knowledge is really obtained, people deemed it possible to write an encyclopedia of all knowledge. So d'Alembert and Diderot did just that from 1751 to 1780. It also seemed possible to construct a nation from scratch without resorting to revelation[20] which is done in the Articles of Confederation in 1781 and redone in 1787 in the Constitution of the United States. An even more drastic construction of a nation follows the French Revolution (1789).

This Age of Enlightenment ushers in the philosophy of Positivism. Positivism canonizes the tenets of the scientific method. Philosophers of this school will assert that not only can we never *know* the answer to any question that deals with what is unobservable or cannot be experienced by the senses, but that such questions are meaningless. Whether God exists is typical of such meaningless questions.

Ironically, almost simultaneous with this school of philosophy, the Romantic Movement flourishes in music, art, and literature and is followed by Impressionism. I say "ironically" because the lush harmonies of a Brahms that give way to the moody, sensual music of a Debussy and the nature poems of Wordsworth that are followed by the sinister symbolism of a Rimbaud appear to be the antithesis of the sterile speculations of the Positivists. But these movements in the arts are simply the other side of the empirical coin; they reflect a worship of this experience from which all knowledge flows.

In 1859 when Darwin published *The Origin of Species*, there was a storm of protest from those who still looked to the Scriptures for their knowledge of all "things human and divine," but the protest does not last long. In a sense, Darwin did for living things what Newton had done for the rest of the universe. He supplied a principle that applies across the board. One could say that Darwin noted about the different species what Laplace had noted about the heavens: God was not needed. Nature accounted for the various species by selecting those strains best adapted to changing conditions in the environment. The peoples of the North Atlantic region could hardly doubt that they were the "fittest"; that they would survive.

Progress was inevitable it seemed. Or, to put it in the vernacular, we were on a roll in the West; we had the key to *scientia*, knowledge. Now we must take on the "white man's burden" and bring this key to the other continents. Here I am suggesting that the imperialism and colonization of the nineteenth century were directly connected to the shift in how we thought we knew reality. There had been conquests and colonization before, in many cases to spread the "faith." But now, in the nineteenth century, these conquests and colonization were to spread the "truth," and we had the technology to do it on a grand scale. However, the century that called its last decade the "Gay Nineties" would have its "truth" subverted soon enough.

SUBVERTING THE ERA OF EXPERIENCE

Undoubtedly, many events contributed to the final shift to pluralism, to the new way we understand how we know. But in this section I concentrate on two: World War I and the New Physics. If World War I crystallized the dead-ended character of the Enlightenment, the new physics *demanded* that we revamp our epistemology or theory of how we know and what we know.

World War I

On June 28, 1914, Archduke Francis Ferdinand of Austria was assassinated, plunging the West and Japan into a war that, except for periodic outbreaks of peace, is a war in which we are still engaged. Some of the principals have changed or changed sides, but the issues that precipitated that conflict (issues of trade, national honor, hostile suspicion) are still operating.

The film *Oh, What a Lovely War* (1969), a surreal rendering of World War I, brings home the particular and peculiar horror of that war. The film begins by depicting the war as an inviting, if typical, British amusement park in the seaside resort of Brighton. "The breezy jingoism of the recruiting songs of the World War I period [are] contrasted with the horrific reality of life in the trenches."[21] No doubt author Joan Littlewood wanted,

46

among other things, to satirize the nineteenth-century wars that were used to make the reputation and careers of countless British colonels. (In the United States, John Hay the secretary of state who presided over the Spanish American War [1898] described that conflict as "a splendid little war!")

The amusement park soon decomposes into a hell-like caricature of amusement as the casualties begin to mount. By the conclusion of the film, the terrible absurdity of those moments in history is forever seared into one's imagination. Almost 17 million members of the military were killed in World War I. Civilian deaths from military action, massacre, starvation, and exposure between 1914 and 1918 are estimated to have been over 12.5 million. Yet rarely did yards or inches of ground change hands. The incomprehensibility of the event shattered the optimism that had prevailed such a short time before. Progress no longer seemed inevitable. World War I was the wind that sowed the whirlwinds of the Jewish Holocaust, the fire bombings of Dresden and Cologne, as well as the nuclear bombing of Hiroshima and Nagasaki in World War II.

As Yeats put it in 1920:

> Things fall apart; the centre cannot hold
> Mere anarchy is loosed upon the world,
> The blood-dimmed tide is loosed, and everywhere
> The ceremony of innocence is drowned;
> The best lack all conviction, while the worst
> Are full of passionate intensity.[22]

The world-wide depression that followed the War-to-End-All-Wars contributed to the malaise that Yeats described. The general conditions of the time fostered a new philosophical school—Existentialism. While there were many variations within this philosophical worldview, Sartre (1905–1980) is the man most often identified as an Existentialist. His answer to an old philosophical question sums up the mood of the era: "Why is there something rather than nothing?" "No reason; existence is absurd!" The arts become self-mocking as reflected in the Theater of the Absurd and perhaps best symbolized by the exhibition of a urinal as sculpture at the famous Armory Art Show (1914) in New York City.

The New Physics

In November 1919, the *New York Times* used the title "A Book for 12 Wise Men" to headline a story about Albert Einstein's theory of relativity. The book referred to was actually only a five-page paper published in a German scientific journal in 1905. The twelve men referred to the fact that so few persons could understand the five pages. And it was not the German language that inhibited the understanding. This was the first reference to Einstein to appear in the *Times*, that chronicler of history, which is to say that for fourteen years the greatest revolution in thinking since Copernicus was all but unknown by most well-read people who were contemporary with the revolution.

Small wonder. In 1911 Paul Langevin, a French physicist, described the implications of relativity in a stunning way. Speaking to a group of philosophers in Bologna, he sketched the impact on twins—one of whom travels to a distant star at almost the speed of light. The other stays home. When the traveling twin returns after two years, two centuries have passed on earth and her sister is long dead.[23]

Throughout Einstein's life, reporters badgered him to explain his theory in terms intelligible to the man and woman in the street. Once he reputedly explained: "We are inclined to think that if all the objects in the universe vanished, there would still be space and time. Well there would not." My favorite story, however, is the one that has Einstein saying, "No, I cannot explain it, but if you come home with me, I'll play it on my violin."[24]

If Copernicus had set us adrift in the skies, Newton at least had tethered us to an absolute space and time. Now this tether was cut. Space and time were relative, dependent on where and when you were. Space and time, which had been thought of as objective properties independent of any entity, were now conceived to be like height, weight, and color. That is, as aspects *of* things. Or more precisely, like height, weight, and color, space and time were also relationships among objects. Our weight, for example, is the relationship between the force of gravity and the mass of the earth. Each of us would weigh in differently on the moon, which has less gravitational pull.

Einstein's theories captured the world's imagination, but other breakthroughs occurred in physics that were hardly less breathtaking. The realization that under some conditions light could be conceived only as waves, but that at other times it must be construed as particles was unnerving to say the least. It could not be both a wave and not a wave. Or could it?

Quantum physics is based on the realization that energy does not appear in a continuous stream but in discrete packets, or quanta. Nothing earth shattering here, it would seem. But then the scientists go on to say that the quanta are either here or there, never in between. It is as if one were to talk about the temperature in a room rising from 70 degrees to 80 degrees without ever passing through the degrees from 71 to 79.

Then there is Heisenberg's law of uncertainty or indeterminacy. It states that one cannot simultaneously determine the location and velocity of particles, not because our instruments are too gross to detect these measurements, but because particles do not have location and velocity at the same time. It was becoming more and more obvious that experience did not deliver reality as it is.

Moreover, accurate predictability, which had been the hallmark of scientific knowledge (the occurrence of a predicted consequence had long been taken as confirmation of a proposed hypothesis), had dissolved into nothing more precise than probability on the subatomic level. The startling feature of these findings was not so much in the findings themselves, stunning as they were. It was the fact that they were occurring in physics, the "hardest" science. The hardness seemed to dissolve further with every breakthrough.

Max Born, a Nobel Prize winner in physics, described the new situation:

> We were taught that there exists an objective physical world, which unfolds itself according to immutable laws independent of us; we are watching this process like the audience watch a

play in the theater. . . . Quantum mechanics
however, interprets the experience in a different
way. We may compare the observer of a physical
phenomenon not with the audience of a
theatrical performance, but with that of a football
game where the act of watching, accompanied by
applauding or hissing, has a marked influence on
the speed and concentration of the players, and
thus on what is watched. In fact, a better simile is
life itself, where audience and actors are the same
persons. It is the action of the experimentalist
who designs the apparatus which determines
essential features of the observations. *Hence, there
is no objectively existing situation, as was supposed
to exist in classical physics.*[25]

What could knowing be in the face of this state of
affairs?

THE NOVELTY OF PLURALISM
Just as the scientific revolutions of the seventeenth
century triggered a desire to distill the method by which
such discoveries were made, so the celebrated
breakthroughs of science in our century triggered a
similar desire, but not so directly. Instead, a whole new
discipline was spawned, the history of science.

In 1950 there were 5 professional historians of
science; twenty years later there were at least 125. And
the field continued to grow. One of the earliest members
of the discipline, Thomas S. Kuhn, published *The
Structure of Scientific Revolutions* in 1962. The book
constituted something of a revolution in itself. Ellen K.

Coughlin, writing in the *Chronicle of Higher Education* twenty years later, noted its phenomenal sales over the years and its wide use as a text book She went on to say that "the book is remarkable for the number and variety of scholars who have written about it, fought over it, borrowed from it, or simply cited it to support their own views."[26] It would be hard to think of a single other book that has had such a significant influence on so many different fields. Anyone who has anything to say about how we know must address Kuhn's findings.

Kuhn begins by using the classical scientific method (observe, hypothesize, experiment, verify) in his study. But what distinguishes Kuhn's work is that conclusions had previously been "drawn, even by scientists themselves, from the study of finished scientific achievements."[27] Kuhn, on the other hand, examines the genesis of these achievements and places them in the scientific context of their times. He concludes that the empirical method found in the textbooks and education of would-be scientists does not correctly identify the way in which major breakthroughs occurred.

Among his findings, the following are most relevant to what knowledge might be:

* Scientists at any particular time constitute a community characterized by a shared set of methods, criteria, and views of the world. He calls these shared values a paradigm. Within this paradigm of reality, scientists work on the problems bequeathed to them by previous generations of their paradigm community.

* Contrary to the popular notion that science proceeds in a value-free and objective context, "evidence" is paradigm dependent. This is why, for example, Columbus could only see India when he landed in the Western Hemisphere. One philosopher of science has summarized the phenomenon this way. "All data are theory laden."[28]

* When a competing paradigm appears on the scene as was the case with the view of the universe proposed by Copernicus, Kuhn claims that those scientists who shift to the new paradigm do so, not as the result of logical argument or irrefutable evidence, but as the result of persuasion and "conversion."[29]

Kuhn illustrated his theory. To Aristotle, watching a pendulum slowing down, the conclusion seems obvious: everything tries to achieve a state of rest. Galileo, some twenty centuries later, watching a similar pendulum sees it as trying to continue its movement. Galileo's "evidence" prepares the paradigm in which Newton can articulate his theory of inertia—that bodies tend to continue at rest or in motion along a straight line until something intervenes to stop them or change their course. In the case of the pendulum, the slowing down is caused by gravity.[30]

Kuhn's theories have been applauded and derided in almost equal measure. "Irrational" was the consensus of the deriders—the kinder ones. Others described the ideas put forth in *The Structure of Scientific Revolutions* as absurd, contradictory, wrong—and in at least one case as immoral![31] He was accused of using the term *paradigm*, a central category in his work, in at least twenty-one different ways.[32] Despite the uproar, however, *paradigm* has passed irretrievably into the conversation within and between disciplines.[33]

Undoubtedly, the terror and fascination that Kuhn's theories have attracted result from the fact that he is forcing us once again to change our notion of knowledge. As arcane and unintelligible as quantum physics and relativity might be to the person on the street, we had confidence in the scientific method as inherited from Bacon. It provided an absolute of sorts. Objective, value-free observation combined with reason and experiment could discover truth. Knowledge, that is justified *true* belief, was still possible. But Kuhn's use of terms like *conversion* and his comparisons (not contrasts) between science and theology undermine that possibility. Philosophers and historians of science have convinced many of us that what we call knowledge is actually only *justified beliefs, projections of the imagination that more or less adequately compel commitment.* But where does that leave us?

THE TEMPTATIONS OF PLURALISM

Three temptations haunt this new era, our era: (a) the denial of pluralism—the refusal to see it as a novel way of being in the world; (b) relativism—one belief or opinion is as good as another; (c) dispassion—a bland, cultural commitment as opposed to passionate embrace of beliefs. In the remainder of these pages, I address these temptations.

54

The Denial of Pluralism

As Einstein remarked, everything has changed but our thinking. It is still possible to think of *pluralism* as another word for tolerance, a description of the fact that we live and work cheek by jowl with people of different, even antithetical, beliefs. Pluralism in this view simply means that we neither persecute these people for their beliefs nor try to impose ours on them. But the implications of tolerance are not explored. In a sense, this entire book is an attempt to help our thinking catch up with the times.

Relativism

Taking pluralism seriously, however, can tempt us into a thoroughgoing skepticism. If so-called knowledge is simply the projections of imagination, are not anyone's imaginative projections as good or as bad as anyone else's? In the next chapter I examine more closely the theories of knowledge and truth that undergird pluralism. I believe such an examination can forestall our succumbing to this temptation.

Dispassion

Taking pluralism seriously can have another effect too. We can find the juice leaking from our beliefs, their life-shaping power weakening. In the second half of this book I speak to this possibility and offer strategies for overcoming the temptation.

CHAPTER TWO

❀

BEYOND RELATIVISM

I t's a free country," shouts the first-grader defending some outrageous statement or behavior, echoing perhaps the equally cogent and persuasive argument of a parent, "Because I said so." Yet if knowledge is in fact a construct of the imagination are not these "reasons" about as cogent and persuasive as one can get? They are if imagination is identified with fantasy. But imagination is not the same as fantasy. In this chapter, I will explore imagination in its role as construing and flavoring our beliefs or interpretations of reality. The role of society and our personal histories will be examined as elements that further complicate our attempts to get beyond relativism. Finally, I will take the bull by the horns and talk about truth and a criteria for justifying beliefs, claiming that the notion of truth and the criteria I propose offer a viable alternative to relativism.

IN THE MATTER OF IMAGINATION

Knowing was such a totally engaging activity for the Israelites that it could include sexual intercourse among its referents. Today we must add the adjective *carnal* to extend *knowledge* that far. Even so, students of knowing have become convinced—or reconvinced—that knowing is not just an activity of mind, but rather of body-mindedness. The imagination best designates the spectrum of body-mind powers with which we compose an experience.[1] In fact, it is the imagination that makes our experience of reality possible by patterning and flavoring our world.

Patterning Reality

Defining reality as "that which is, the way that it is" or "whatever exists as it exists," we sense that we have not said much. "A booming, buzzing confusion"[2] has content closer to our experience. Yet on our better days, we do not experience reality that way either. We experience it as patterned, as a discrete set of things and relationships. The things may be grim and the relationships may be tragic, but they are *there*. Or are they? Where do the patterns come from? Max Born, as well as others cited in the last chapter, suggest that we project them on reality.

I am told that the first vision of persons born blind whose sight is restored is of a wash of color. They do not see things; they do not see a chair with a lamp behind it; they do not see foregrounds and backgrounds but simply a confusion of radiances. They must learn to pattern chair and lamp and background and foreground and red out of that confusion. We forget that we do not see chairs or red either. I have used the following approach to make the case that *experience is our interaction with reality AFTER it has been patterned or netted by imagination.*

Remember the question in Philosophy or Psychology 101? "Does the tree that falls in the forest make a noise if there is no ear to hear it?" Some of us may forget the answer: No. We can refute arguments that invoke a forest existence of tape recorders and the like by whipping out a transistor radio. Tuning in the music and talk shows dramatizes the fact that the availability of experiences depends upon the appropriate equipment. A sensation requires both a stimulus *and* a sensor. The next step is to recognize that we almost never have a "raw" or pure sensation; it is always interpreted. Consider the following: △ To the question "What do you see?" people usually begin by answering "a triangle." But a triangle is a very sophisticated mathematical concept; you cannot really *see* that." Then people say, "Three lines." But again, "three" is a high level abstraction and lines are series of points having length but no breadth. And points are geometric elements that have position but no size, shape, or extension. Now who can *see* that or those? The point here, of course, is that we cannot say what we see the way we see it; the sight is always interpreted: we always see *as*—a triangle, *as* three lines.

In other words our experience of reality is mediated by interpretive schemes. Experience is not simply interaction with our environment (including ourselves) but is our *interpreted* interaction. The imagination casts a kind of netting upon reality. Not that we do not experience reality, we do.[3] What we experience, however, is not so much the nature of the ooze-through but the shape, measurement, and imprint of the netting.

The work of cartographers provides an analogy. The lines of latitude and longitude with which they mark our maps are obviously a construct of human imagination. (There are no lines in the Pacific ocean—or anywhere else for that matter.) But this netting makes it possible to know where we are and to get where we are going. Just so, the patterning of all of reality enables us to know where we are and get where we are going.

FLAVORING REALITY

While the patterning or netting function of imagination may appear to be more closely related to the mind of body-mindedness, the flavoring function demonstrably involves the body. It is almost as if our models or patterns or imaginative constructs have sensible qualities; as if they have aromas, tastes, textures, colors, and perhaps even sounds that more or less appeal to us.

As the ear shapes the sound, and our taste buds give us sour, sweet, bitter, and salty, so our imagination flavors our constructs in ways that cause us to be attracted or repelled by what we experience. It is this function of the imagination that politicians pander to in election years. We refer to it as "the image." But it is not so much a picture to which we react as it is a composite of picture, smell, taste, and sound communicated by the way the vote-seeker comes through our netting—the "feel" of the candidate.

Much of these netting patterns and flavorings come from society and our individual backgrounds. Original netting and flavoring is rare. When we experience it, we call it creativity. Awareness of the predisposing elements in our perception of reality can prevent their having a stranglehold on our experience, can put some play into the netting of our interpretations, can contribute to our creativity.

THE ROLE OF SOCIETY IN NETTING REALITY

Language is perhaps the most obvious instance of society's netting of reality. Words are human constructions. In *The Oxford English Dictionary*, we can follow the derivation and entrance of words into English. In our own lifetimes we see words emerge (*robot*) and fade (*thee* and *thy*) and change meaning. In the King James version of the Bible *let* meant hinder and *prevent* meant precede. Yet as loose and living as our language is, we have to learn it. We study and learn language the way we study and learn chemistry.

In other words, although we recognize that any particular language is a human creation, the projection of a society, the language in turn shapes us and dictates how we must use it. The rules of language, for example, reflect arbitrary agreements. Like the number of feet between bases on a baseball diamond, the rules can be changed at any time if a significant number of interested parties agree to the change. But until they are changed, you are judged "wrong" if you use a verb tense incorrectly. Just as a baseball player is out if he stops five feet before the base, no matter how convinced he is that the bases should only be eighty-five feet apart.

The examples from language and baseball also illustrate the situation that, alone, we cannot introduce a novel or changed netting scheme into the mix. Peter L. Berger and Thomas Luckmann, authors of *The Social Construction of Reality*, refer to the circumstance that we cannot sustain a solitary interpretation as the need for plausibility structures, that is, a community of persons who will support our proposed interpretation.[4] To invent words for which no one else knows the meaning is to engage in a futile exercise. Similarly, to "discover" a law of physics that no one else supports is to forego the possibility of publication so that potential believers cannot even be rounded up. In our own day, it is also to forego funding, which makes the accumulation of credibility through validating experiments an impossibility.

Berger and Luckmann could have entitled their book *The Volley Ball Syndrome*. Reality is a ball kept in play by a team of believers. As the believers fall away, perhaps to play in another game, perhaps to leave the game altogether in death, the ball is kept aloft with more and more difficulty until it is finally dropped and often judged by those in other games never to have been "real" in the first place. Max Planck, who introduced the notion of energy as quanta, wrote in his autobiography, "A new scientific truth does not triumph by convincing its opponents and making them see the light, but rather because its opponents eventually die, and a new generation grows up that is familiar with it."[5] The new generation then concludes that the opponents had been playing bad science all along.

We bring some awareness to our incorporation of the conventions that we call language or baseball or physics. There are other conventions, however, that seem to seep into our socialization, into the shaping and flavoring of our nets. Paradoxically, these cultural conventions seem to exercise more power over our interaction with reality than those of which we are aware.

Why should eating cat, for example, disturb us anymore than eating chicken? No reason. Yet I have seen people become physically ill at the prospect. In our culture, we do not eat cat. Moreover, I would wager that if a Gallop poll were to be taken asking people which they would rather be accused of—being irreligious or smelling bad (here *irreligious* could be replaced by lying, stealing, adultery, perhaps even murder) I would wager that a large majority would choose irreligious. In our culture, cleanliness is not next to godliness, it supersedes godliness. Yet cleanliness is a relatively recent value and *smelling* clean, even more recent.

THE INDIVIDUAL'S CONTRIBUTION TO THE NETTING OF REALITY

In addition to society's input to our experience of reality, we also bring our unique netting system to interpretation in the forms of our genetic structure, our past, our current beliefs, and our commitments.

Genetic Structure

No two sets of fingerprints are alike. The pattern of our prints on everything we touch symbolizes the uniqueness of the way we touch the world. We are not usually as aware of the converse: that the world touches us through that pattern too. All our experience bears our unique imprint. What we hear, what we taste, what we see is filtered through this original relation to the universe.

But the genetic influence on our experience is not limited just to sensation. Whether we are genetically predisposed to have a surplus of fat cells will determine to a large extent how we interact with the world—at least three times a day every day of our lives. Our genes even suggest the way we will experience death by making us more susceptible to some diseases rather than others.

Studies of identical twins separated at birth suggest that our knowledge of genes is on the verge of a breakthrough. Apparently, our genetic nature accounts for more of our traits and attitudes than we had ever imagined.[6]

The Past and Present

Through the years we continue to shape our uniqueness in the choices that we make, the memories that we entertain, the beliefs we hold, and the commitments we embrace. Our choices, like a sculptor's chisel, chip away at our possibilities until a shape emerges. As we age, the shape hardens. Our choices diminish in number and extent as possibility disappears. So a person who has chosen a career as an accountant must come to grips with the fact that she or he will never see the world as an astronaut does. Our choices shape what we see and when we see it.

Our memories also shape what we experience. They lure or repel us in certain directions according to the flavor of the memory. A man may decide to include certain disciplines in the way he raises his child as a result of memories of his own childhood. A woman may decide not to become a physician because of sad memories of an absent parent physician.

Our beliefs and commitments similarly direct and color our experience. Only people who believe that miracles can happen will see miracles; nonbelievers will see an up-to-now inexplicable phenomenon. As one commentator phrased it, "When I believe it, I'll see it."[7] Commitments can create experience from scratch. The commitment to build a new bridge is fundamental to the possibility of ever experiencing that bridge. This truism applies to all kinds of bridge-building, all kinds of commitments.

RELATIVISM REVISITED

The discussion so far has done little to add to our confidence that we can get beyond relativism. If in fact knowledge is one's imagination patterning and flavoring reality, how can we determine which patternings and flavorings deserve our belief? Is knowledge simply a convention like eating chicken instead of cat? "It's a free country" as they say. Does that mean we are free to believe whatever we wish?

What has become problematic in the definition of knowledge as justified true belief was its specifying note: true. If the reliability of knowledge can be salvaged, it depends on the possibility of justifying beliefs. But before engaging in a salvaging operation, we should examine what we have lost when we have lost truth. If, in fact, we have lost it.

MODELS OF TRUTH

Our most common notion of truth goes by the name "correspondence theory." If I say, "It is raining outside," and that corresponds to what is happening, I am said to have spoken *the* truth (pronounced thee). Trees falling in forests notwithstanding, this model of truth is very helpful in the dailiness of our lives. Using it we are able to determine whether children are lying when they say they are not chewing gum and whether spouses are telling the truth when they claim to be faithful. In that sense the correspondence theory of truth is like Euclidean geometry which enables us to navigate the planet well enough but is not adequate to space travel. In the larger picture, the correspondence theory is inadequate too. Actually, it is also inadequate in the smaller picture, but negligibly so.

Once we forego the possibility of access to reality as it is, we simultaneously forego the possibility of comparing our interpretations with the real thing. The consensus on what constitutes rain, however, is sufficiently universal—and perhaps trivial—that we can check the truth of the statement "It is raining" by using the model of correspondence without anxiety.

As the issues get larger, the capacity of the correspondence method to get at the truth diminishes proportionately. For example, the model of spousal faithfulness in most Western societies is that of monogamy. But that is not the model of fidelity in every society. Therefore a yes or no to the question of faithfulness is, as Kuhn might say, "paradigm dependent." Explanations of this type are not recommended, however, when a simple yes or no is called for by one's spouse.

The correspondence theory of truth is even less adequate as we get into implications and meaning. Even in the examples above one would be hard put to discern the true implications of the gum chewing. Is this activity a conscious rebellion, or is it the thoughtlessness of youth in one who forgot to empty her or his mouth before entering the classroom? What difference does it make? We must make judgments because we must act or not act according to what we decide. But the judgment and the follow-up must be made without certainty. After Freud, we realize that even the offending child cannot interpret the activity or its meaning with certainty.

If this is the case with gum chewing how much more significant is the lack of certainty with regard to infidelity. Having gotten the "truth" from the unfaithful spouse, how shall this be interpreted? What difference does it make? Is this a fling that will not be repeated, or is this the end of the marriage? Actions must be taken either to work at shoring up the marriage or terminating it, but they must be taken with the agonizing recognition that one has no certainty about the interpretation or its meaning or the appropriateness of the actions about to be taken.

And that is the rub. The major casualty of the inadequacy of the correspondence model of truth is certainty and, even worse, the possibility of certainty.

In our heart of hearts we always knew that we did not have certainty with regard to life-shaping choices, decisions, interpretations. We always realized in our depths that our choice of this school or this job or this spouse was based on uncertain "knowledge." And it was precisely this lack of certainty that convinced us that the discernment of implications and meanings was not scientific, that is not *really* knowledge in the sense of justified true beliefs, was not *scientia*. Certainty was the note that distinguished the arts from the sciences.

History could offer justified beliefs and literature could offer provocative and life-enhancing insights, but the sciences could offer certainty. In fact they were arranged on a scale according to the degree of certainty they could offer. On the lower end of the scale were the social sciences. They were considered *soft* and sometimes dismissed as being "arts" by those on the upper, *harder* end of the scale, those in the physical sciences.[8] An economist cannot predict that inflation will follow full employment with the same certainty that a physicist can predict that if you let go of this book it will fall towards the floor.

When physicists begin to talk as Max Born did in the last chapter (". . . there is no objectively existing situation") and when philosophers and historians of science begin to interpret and suggest the meaning of such talk, certainty does not survive the conversation. As a result, the sciences, particularly at the theoretical level, are beginning more and more to look like the arts. An indication of this is the use of terminology from the arts in the sciences. For example: the most fundamental constructs of matter have been named quarks (from literature), different quarks are called beauty, strange, and charm (from aesthetics), allusion is made to "the eightfold path" (from the Buddhist tradition). Max Bohr's words no longer surprise us: "When it comes to atoms, language can be used only as in poetry. The poet, too, is not nearly so concerned with describing facts as with creating images."[9]

Again, as we might suspect, the realization that we do not have direct access to reality and that therefore we cannot have certainty about our interpretations of this reality did not blow full-blown in the twentieth century. Shortly before his death, Galileo wrote to a friend:

> The falsity of the Copernican system must not on any account be doubted. . . . God being able to do in many or rather infinite ways, that which to our view and observation seems to be done in one particular way, we must not pretend to hamper God's hand and tenaciously maintain that in which we may be mistaken. And just as I deem inadequate the Copernican observations and conjectures, so I judge equally, and more, fallacious and erroneous those of Ptolemy, Aristotle, and their followers, when even without going beyond the human bounds of human reasoning their inconclusiveness can be very easily discovered.[10]

Somehow, Galileo anticipated the following observations of a physicist:

> The Inquisition and Galileo agreed on one point only, that there was a definite question to be answered, as to whether the sun or the earth was at rest, and that they were both wrong. For on the theory of relativity the sun is no more a center of absolute rest than is the earth and *the whole system of the planets could be worked out just as*

correctly starting from the supposition that the earth was at rest. It so happens that, owing to the immense mass of the sun, the mathematics is much simpler, much more convenient if the sun be taken as at rest, but we know that, even considering a framework supplied by the so-called fixed stars, it is not.[11]

If anything, the discussion so far seems to strengthen the case for relativism. If one cannot be certain, if the Copernican and Ptolemaic theories are interchangeable or both wrong, perhaps we should embrace the position that one theory, one interpretation, one articulation of meaning is as good as another. Even if one is better than another, we cannot know which one with certainty, so we would be wise to treat them as equally valuable. Wrong!

In fact, the validity of the correspondence version of truth was questioned by scientists and philosophers even during the era when knowledge was based on experience, or rather, because knowledge was based on experience. If *scientia* (true beliefs) was based on experience and demonstrated by certainty of predictions, there was a problem. How could one say with certainty that all crows are black unless one had experienced all crows? There was always the possibility that over the next mountain a green crow was lurking. The problem of induction was the name given to our inability to generalize with certainty no matter how many instances we had experienced. The problem gnawed at philosophers particularly. Most scientists do not have the luxury of time or the inclination of temperament to reflect on how they make coffee or discover reality. What has emerged from the philosophical studies as the most viable model of truth is one that has been around a long time.

THE HEBREW MODEL OF TRUTH

The correspondence theory of truth is the most common notion of truth as we use the term in our conversation. But it is not the only one. Truth in the correspondence theory is a Greek concept that should not surprise us because *scientia* and science are Greek gifts to the West. Hebrew does not have an equivalent for *truth* in the Greek or correspondence sense. The Hebrew word *emet* is probably closer to the Anglo Saxon etymology of *true*, which most lexicographers see as *drew* or tree referring to the firmness of the tree. In other words, to be true was to be dependable, to be faithful. The relation of truth to trust in this theory is more than the obvious visible resemblance. To "plight one's troth" is Middle English for pledging one's truth, that is, one's fidelity, one's trustworthiness.

In this Hebrew theory, an interpretation, a meaning, *acquires* truth, becomes more and more credible, that is, more and more believable. Verification (literally: making true) is not a once-and-for-all exercise; it is an ongoing activity in which an interpretation accumulates credit or, as it were, trustworthiness. The process is not unlike the way we acquire a good credit rating: we do so by coming through in a creditable way every time we are put to the test by the presentation of a bill. Even after a bankruptcy, we are likely to be able to find someone who will give us credit, who will trust us. So a failure of the evidence does not necessarily falsify an interpretation. However, a pattern of failures like a pattern of bankruptcies, while never establishing with certainty the falseness of the model of reality or the untrustworthiness of a would-be borrower, makes both less and less creditable.

Circumstances work to persuade or dissuade us of the truthfulness in the sense of trustworthiness of an interpretation. Which is to say that verification is neither automatic nor arbitrary. It is the obvious arbitrariness of the position that one opinion is as good as another that repels us. Also its irrationality. To hold that one opinion is as good as another is to say simultaneously that holding the opinion that some opinions are better than others is also a valid opinion!

The Hebrew model of truth requires time, history, for the verification process to unfold. But even to initiate the verification process, we must commit ourselves to the possibility of truth. For example, one must actually marry to allow the value of the marriage to work itself out in time; one must commit oneself to the research program to learn of its validity down the line. There must be criteria therefore that help us to judge the prospective truth of an interpretation of reality. I turn to those criteria now.

EVALUATING INTERPRETATIONS OF REALITY

The eras of knowing described in the first chapter (knowledge as revelation and knowledge as experience) contained in their descriptions the criteria for evaluating the interpretations of reality. In the first era, the criterion was correspondence to revelation. In the second, the criterion was correspondence to experience. In both these ages, at least on the face of it, the criteria were outside the evaluator. That is, the criteria are what we usually call "objective." To describe knowledge as imaginative constructs seems to condemn us to the most subjective of criteria—imagination. But we have criteria that have been used to judge imaginative constructs through all the ages, namely aesthetic criteria.

I submit that the interpretations we cast across reality are art objects. Let me commandeer the support of two outstanding philosophers of aesthetic theory to make my case. Suzanne Langer describes art, the activity and the product, as "the creation of perceptible form expressive of human feeling."[12] But imaginative constructs, the patterning and flavoring that compose our beliefs, can also be described as "perceptible forms expressive of human feeling."

John Dewey's contribution to the case is that of questioning our ordinary notion of art. In his book *Art as Experience*, he argues against limiting art to what we find in museums or concert halls. He tries to "restore the continuity between the refined and intensified forms of experience that are works of art"[13] and the more common everyday forms we project against reality to deliver our experience. According to Dewey, the interpretations that we have traditionally called art are to all interpretations what mountain peaks are to the earth. "Mountain peaks do not float unsupported; they do not even rest upon the earth. They *are* the earth in one of its manifest operations."[14] So there are symphonies and super string theories that interpret our existence. And there are theories of marriage and child-rearing that are perceptible forms expressing human feeling. Dewey says art is what it does with and in experience. Our interpretive schemes give us the form and content of our experience more or less artfully.

The equation of interpretations of reality with art is helpful for several reasons. First, we do not expect our works of art to deliver reality as it is. But we do expect them to deliver it in a way that makes us experience reality in transformed ways, in significant ways, in ways that change the manner of our seeing and hearing.

Moreover, the rejection of relativism is central to aesthetic theory. There is a long tradition of criticizing art works, of recognizing that one piece of art or one performance is not necessarily as good as another. There is also a tradition that extends back even farther than art criticism that somehow the good, the true, and the beautiful are three variations on the same theme, three interpretations of the same reality.

Finally there is a tentativeness in art criticism. One evaluates a work of art at one's peril. A careful and impassioned judgment that here is beauty or truth or goodness may be displaced by subsequent judgments of others and even of one's own. The words *certainty* and *eternal* are not likely to be found in critical reviews.

Evaluation implies desirability. In evaluating, we try to discover the worth or worthiness of an interpretation of reality whether it is a painting, a religious ritual, or the plank of a political party. My thesis is that the aesthetic mode of evaluation offers the most fruitful approach to estimating the value of any interpretation.

Aesthetic evaluation draws on our best thinking and our most cultivated sensibilities. It is, if you will, reasoned feeling and feeling reason, a focused application of our body-mindedness. The notion of "thoughtfulness"[15] crystallizes this reasoned feeling. Through the prism of thoughtfulness, therefore, I will lay out an aesthetic check list.

THE THOUGHTFUL STANCE

To describe someone as thoughtful can simply refer to a person's having a pensive disposition. But we usually mean something more imaginative and active. Consider *thoughtful* in relation to gifts and gift-giving. In designating a gift or a gift-giver as thoughtful, the ability to bring at least three perspectives to bear on one's judgment seems to be present, namely the perspectives of intimacy, distance, and community.

The Perspective of Intimacy

Contrary to traditional lore, love is not blind; defensive and defending perhaps, but not blind. Who knows us better than someone who loves us? Who is more equipped to evaluate music than someone who loves it? Love energizes us to learn all that we can learn about a person, all that we can learn about a discipline, about a God. Love enables us to examine what we have learned in the best light. When purchasing clothes whose color we wish to determine "for sure," we sometimes leave the artificial light of the salesroom to study the color in natural light. It is unlikely that we will ever again be wearing the clothes in that exact light, yet there is a sense in which in the natural light we have discerned the true (meaning most dependable) color. So, too, loving persons, music, political platforms is like seeing people and things in the best light.

From the perspective of intimacy, thoughtfulness sympathetically scans what is loved for intimations of the fitting. What gift would this person enjoy, use, be happily surprised to receive? Reasoning and creative imagination evaluate the situation. A beloved child might be wonderfully surprised and pleased to receive a 44 Magnum revolver as a present, but I presume loving parents would reason out such a gift.

The Perspective of Distance

Our sound and sight equipment enables us to hear and see up close and from a distance, simultaneously teaching us that neither perspective is the whole sound or the whole picture. A violinist immersed in the string section of a symphony orchestra does not hear the same piece of music that the conductor or the audience hears. Distance acts as a kind of displacement mechanism. It rescues us from the single-sidedness of intimacy and immersion, straining our netting into new shapes so that new facets of reality are glimpsed. Creation in a grain of sand is the same creation seen in pictures of our fragile planet spinning through space, but from the perspective of distance. Thoughtfulness requires that we get as many perspectives as possible.

The Perspective of Community

A most fruitful interpretation of reality at this time hypothesizes that things do not have relationships; they *are* their relationships. Persons are not related to other persons and to the environment; they emerge from their relatedness; they are a form of their environment—including other persons. If, for example, I cannot maintain my relatedness to the planet, incorporating it in carrots and tomatoes, making carrots and tomatoes into me, I will literally shrivel up and blow away. My personhood must be sustained by human exchanges just as my bodily existence thrives on the carrot-tomato exchange with the earth. Ecology is the study of reality as a web.

William James said that anything that makes a difference anywhere, makes a difference everywhere. We experience that insight in new and at times terrifying ways. The destruction of rain forests in South America extends the desert and the inevitability of starvation in Africa. The use of aerosol hair sprays in our bathrooms eats away at the ozone layer that protects us from lethal sun rays. The thousands of years of shelf life in the nuclear waste that we are burying in our planet threatens generations beyond our imagination—generations of everything: rhinos, mosquitoes, carrots, tomatoes, and people.

It is not enough therefore to evaluate from the perspective of intimacy and distance; we must also bring to bear our embeddedness. The fact is that, like it or not, we are communal beings, in absolute relatedness to our environment, the whole galaxy of it. Thoughtfulness requires that any evaluating activity must be launched from this perspective.

Having described the stances from which we should look *at* any interpretation of reality, let me suggest here what we should be looking *for.* I will use John Dewey's criteria for evaluating an aesthetic experience as reference points, namely, conservation, tension, culmination, fulfillment.[16] Expectation dominates and pervades these criteria.

EXPECTATION

We bring a whole set of expectations reflecting our education and tastes to any interpretation of reality. For example, we may expect from our poetry: word imagery, sensuousness, emotional intensity, economy, story interest, depth of thought, power, and so on. We bring different expectations to a theory in physics. Yet, some overlapping occurs. Economy, in the sense of explaining the maximum with the least complication, might be expected of a physical theory too.

These expectations peculiar to genres of interpretation (painting, economic theory, morality, to name some genres) are framed in the light of what we expect the interpretation to be or, more accurately, to do. What is the purpose of this interpretative scheme? Which is to say, what is its meaning (the difference we expect it to make)? Poetry and physics obviously have different immediate meanings. Yet all expectations are related at a deeper level because there is an overriding purpose to all interpretations of reality, namely, the enhancement of existence. I propose that existence is enhanced as the perspectives from which we experience are extended and deepened.

Intimacy

Say that I especially enjoy the work of this poet whose new poem is before me. I have studied and am familiar with her symbol system, her allusions, and her poetic forms; I love her work. I am able to bring an informed, ensouled consciousness to the work. I can examine it from the perspective of intimacy. As I study the new poem, it extends my knowledge of her symbol system, allusions, and poetic forms and deepens my appreciation and enthusiasm for her entire body of work. I can go back to older poems more intimately prepared to appraise and enjoy them. My capacity to experience them has been enhanced.

Distance

If I am only familiar with this poet's poetry, if I cannot bring the perspective of distance, my experience is constricted. I cannot experience the pleasure of comparing and contrasting, the taste of intimations of which the poet herself may be unaware. But an extended familiarity with the work of other poets, from other ages and from other cultures, simultaneously enhances my experience of this poet and the work at issue extends and deepens the distance from which I can appreciate all poetry in the future.

Community

Finally, as we bring our embeddedness to bear on the poem, it should enliven our sense of relatedness, minimally by putting us inside the experience of the poet, maximally in its rendering of particularity extending and deepening the experience of our utter relatedness beyond me and the poet. Shakespeare's poetry has apparently done this for generations and for all kinds of people. He enables us to identify not just with Hamlet and Portia, but with the Hamlet and Portia dimension in all relationships.

CONSERVATION

Conservation might be described as equivalent to the medical and ethical injunction: first, do no harm. We must at least be able to bring the perspectives of intimacy, distance, and embeddedness to the judgment. If the poem is in an unknown language or the vocabulary so esoteric that one cannot get close to it, evaluation is impossible. On the other hand, if there is no novelty, no displacement such that one can get some distance from the familiar, the interpretation must be judged to be "flat," literally. Finally, the interpretation should not tear at our embeddedness. Some of the Surrealist art of the thirties, in which women rarely had faces, appeared frequently as a mannequin and on a pedestal or in chains seems to me to tear at our embeddedness. And any interpretation that tears at our embeddedness is legitimately judged obscene whether we are talking about an economic theory to support prices that pay farmers not to grow crops while people starve, or a medical theory that enjoins the farming of human fetal cells for their curative powers.

TENSION

The simultaneous promotion of the three perspectives will create a tension in any profound interpretation of reality. Perfect balance is probably never achieved, perhaps not even desirable. Without the vitality generated by the various perspectives straining to engage our experience in this or that interpretation, we must judge the interpretation to be lifeless. A poem may appeal because it names our private life with exquisite precision. Or it may appeal because it is so novel in execution as to be fascinating. Or it may appeal because its pitch for embeddedness is so engaging as to border on propaganda. Artful interpretations of reality will reflect the tension in our existence to promote all three perspectives authentically.

CUMULATION

This feature of an interpretation of reality is a form of verification. As we become more familiar with the interpretation (whether a poem, a moral directive, or a religious dogma), as time lends distance to its initial appearance, as it passes into the tissues of the culture, if it continues to illuminate existence and enhance experience, it accumulates credibility.

FULFILLMENT

Expectation, conservation, tension, and cumulation as criteria are not unique to aesthetic experience. But fulfillment is. The "Ahh," the "It is enough," the sense of consummation, the realization that not everything is a means to an end but that some things are ends in themselves is some kind of supreme enhancement of existence. Few interpretations of reality meet this criterion, yet I would argue that it is precisely this experience or the promise of it that generates commitment to an interpretation of reality. It is also at the heart of any change in commitment to an interpretation of reality.

RELIGIOUS PLURALISM REVISITED

In the last chapter, I set out the "problem of pluralism" as a temptation to relativism. I tried to trace how we arrived through intolerance and tolerance to pluralism by tracking the different ways we have conceived knowledge. I have argued that the criteria we have traditionally brought to imaginative constructs, that is, aesthetic criteria, offer the most fruitful approach to the evaluation of knowledge as imagining. Can these criteria be legitimately applied to religious interpretations of reality?

The prospect of evaluating religious traditions seems a little nervy to say the least. But hubris is only one of the problems involved in examining a religion according to human criteria. There is first of all the uniqueness of religion. How can one apply aesthetic criteria to a way of life? Another problem is the variety of traditions within any particular religion. Yet another is the difficulty of gaining the perspectives recommended in the last section. And yet . . .

The Uniqueness of Religion

Religious interpretations of reality differ from others not so much by reason of their content, as by reason of their extension. Religions, that is, are not concerned with one or even several aspects of reality, but with the whole of reality, offering explanations of all that is, the meaning and value of everything. How can we compare a religious tradition with a symphony, a super-string theory, or a model of marriage? Religion is so thoroughly encompassing. A symphony, a super-string theory and even a model of marriage interpret only aspects of our existence. But religion is the framework within which we aspire to write symphonies, pursue the secrets of the universe, and critique our models of marriage. Religion, as Cantwell Smith says, does not mean something, it confers meaning.[17]

The Variety Within a Religious Tradition

Within any particular religious tradition we can mark significant changes in that religion, not only through the centuries, but in its embodiment from culture to culture, from city to rural areas. In a remarkable book, Jaroslav Pelikan has traced the different images of *Jesus Through the Centuries*.[18] Looking at the diverse characteristics of Christianity's central figure, we are bound to question, "Which characterization shall we evaluate?"

About Perspectives

The perspective of community is the least problematic stance from which we can launch an evaluation. It is relatively easy to determine the degree and manner in which a religion protects and promotes our embeddedness in the universe. Intimacy allows us to probe our religion with a loving eye. But that same intimacy almost precludes our looking at another religion with the same loving critique. Love of Brahms does not rule out love of Beethoven. On the contrary, such dual allegiance in the arts undoubtedly deepens both loves. But intimacy with a tradition from which we draw the very meaning of our lives would seem to preclude, or at least make very difficult, a loving appreciation of another frame of meaning.

The opposite circumstance prevails when we try to obtain distance. If we find that getting inside another religion is hard, we find it equally difficult to get outside our own. By definition, religion is all-encompassing, so where would we go to be "at a distance"?

About Hubris

Even if the other difficulties could be overcome, is it not some supreme insolence to assemble our critical tools before the nettings that claim to manifest the Deity? It is, if we collapse the difference between the religious traditions and the Deity they claim to mediate: if the religious tradition and God are interchangeable; if our religion is God. In this case, however, the problem is idolatry not hubris.

It is our power to reflect and to evaluate that makes our commitments—even commitment to God—human. We are not vegetables that must gravitate toward the sun. We are persons whose power to choose the demonic as well as the Godly demonstrates our vocation to appraise choices.

We must, therefore, make judgments. But factoring in the difficulties I have outlined will make our judgments of religion especially tentative. All to the good, I think. The opposite of relativism is not a ranking system.[19] Rather, it is the conviction that some interpretations of reality are better than others and that criteria exist that can act as clues for discerning the better—not with certainty, but, at least, with some warrant. I have set out what those criteria might look like.

Let me advise the reader that applying these criteria to the major world religions will not automatically rule out an entire religion, though the activity may identify those elements in a religious tradition which are ugly or immoral, that is, irreligious. But our chief concern has to be discerning the religious and irreligious elements in our own religion. Identification with a religious tradition intensifies the responsibility to question that tradition above all others.

EXPECTATIONS OF RELIGION

Every religion expects certain behaviors, beliefs, and practices from its adherents. What should adherents expect from religion? What every religion promises: enhanced existence. Called salvation in most Western religions, and liberation and enlightenment in Eastern religions, religions are quite up front in proposing a corrected and more profound experience of reality to its members.

We can ask ourselves, therefore, to what degree does my tradition extend and deepen my capacity for intimacy, distance, and community? Where are the elements of conservation, tension, cumulation to be found? Where is the fulfillment?

There is a rub to the exercise, however. As previously stated, evaluation is most favorably launched from an intimate, a loving perspective. Yet that perspective is precisely the one that pluralism seems to undermine. Our beliefs are fragile when they are unsupported by the total culture. Conviction is hard to come by when certainty is an impossibility. Participation in a religious tradition these days, therefore, is likely to be nominal. I will address this state of affairs in the following chapters.

❀

CHAPTER THREE

CONVERSION

"Tolerance is the virtue of people who do not believe anything."[1] Chesterton, who wrote this, is wrong of course. We can think of fanatical believers who, perhaps because they are a minority, tolerate the different beliefs of the majority in their community. Yet, there is a haunting nugget of insight in Chesterton's declaration. We might make that insight explicit by this less pithy, but more accurate rewording: "In a pluralistic atmosphere, the life's blood of people's beliefs frequently drains away."

We are tempted to dispassion. Perhaps *tempted* is too dramatic, suggesting a conscious attraction. Our religious beliefs are more likely to fade unnoticed and unmourned, unless and until some crisis jolts us. Without the conviction of certainty and without a confirming consensus, our religious faith can degenerate to mere ceremonial significance.[2] Studies show that our economic status, educational level and general lifestyle, not our religion, determine how we live. The people next door may hold beliefs antithetical to ours, but for purposes of political polls or TV Neilsen ratings, we are indistinguishable from them.

This chapter is about conversion as the dynamic that enables us to believe passionately. It is also about God's role and our role in precipitating the kind of conversion I am talking about.

KINDS OF CONVERSION

Conversion: Builders do it when they make an old mansion into condominiums; fourth graders when they change fractions into decimals; quarterbacks when they call third-down plays that work. In its earliest usages *conversio* meant both the revolution of the celestial bodies and a person's turning to God.[3] More recently, in the realm of the personal, conversion has been described simply and succinctly as "a human mechanism for conflict resolution that is often set in a religious context."[4] Understood this way, a conversion can be vertical or horizontal, religious in the conventional and ecclesiastical sense or in a looser way.

VERTICAL AND HORIZONTAL CONVERSIONS

A new discipline, stage, or developmental theory has been carved out of psychology, biology, ethics, and religious studies. Its proponents claim that, just as the physical growth of children conforms to patterns making it possible to predict when a child will be able to sit up and walk and talk, we can similarly track stages in human reasoning powers, moral thinking, and faith development. Such development is frequently referred to as a vertical movement. Concentrating on this vertical development, James Fowler, a contemporary stage theorist, treats faith as a verb, the activity by which we shape our lives in relation to more or less comprehensive convictions or assumptions about reality.[5]

Using the work of the other developmental theorists, Fowler studies the structure and stages that ground the shaping of our world views. He traces the developing capacities (structures) for faithing and the actualization of those capacities (stages). For example: our increasing ability to reason or to appreciate the perspective of others can contribute to a more nuanced and richer faithing. When this happens, we move to another stage in faith development. Some commentators describe such movement as a vertical conversion.[6] Young people who become capable of *personally* appropriating the religious faith in which their parents nurtured them—and do, in fact, appropriate that faith—reflect such a conversion.

For Fowler, such movement is not conversion. He is quite explicit: conversion does not refer to the vertical movement through the stages; conversion is horizontal.[7] It occurs not in the *way* we believe, but in the *what* or the content of our beliefs.

Fowler specifies the content of faith as centers of value, images of power, and master stories. The centers of value are the concerns that either consciously or unconsciously we consider worthy of shaping our lives. The images of power include the powers with which we align ourselves, for example, the power of nonviolence or the power of nuclear deterrence. The master stories are those narratives—perhaps even proverbs—we tell ourselves that articulate our interpretation of existence. A person whose life is shaped by the story "I am my sister and my brother's keeper" will have a different faith life from someone whose master story is "There's no such thing as a free lunch." A change in one or more of these contents—the values that center our lives or the images or powers with which we align ourselves or the master stories we tell ourselves—constitutes a conversion. And, in fact, most studies of conversion concentrate on the content changes of our believing.

An exhaustive study, however, by Walter E. Conn describes conversion as both vertical and horizontal. He focuses on conscience as the dynamism of conversion and, paradoxically, conversion as the transformation of conscience. Our developing capacities are the condition of this transformation. Conscience creates our "second nature" or character as a particular "sort of person"[8] As such, it involves both structure and content. For example: "Moral conversion is not first of all a choosing of new values (content), but choosing value as the criterion of one's choice"—a structural change.[9]

The kinds of conversion described above need not be religious in the cultural or institutional sense. Many people shape their lives in terms of convictions and assumptions not ordinarily considered religious. Paul Tillich spoke of God as our Ultimate Concern. Turn this around and whatever concerns us ultimately is god for us. This being concerned ultimately is another way to speak of being religious, of worshipping. We would hope that the object of our concern is worthy of our attitude.

(*Worship* is historically as well as visibly related to *worthy*.) Since our conscience (Conn) or our "centers of value, images of power and master stories" (Fowler) do, in fact, define what is worthy for us, any changes in these elements can legitimately be called religious conversions. In Mario Puzo's *The Godfather*,[10] Michael's transformation from a disinterested observer of his father's machinations into a brutal Mafia chief is a religious conversion, if a demonic one. Unfortunately, conversion is a neutral mechanism for resolving conflict.

CONVERSION IN THE PLURALISTIC CONTEXT

The kind of conversion I will consider in this section is religious in the more conventional sense, that is, it has to do with God and God's relationship to the world. But it is neither the horizontal nor the vertical type of conversion, though those two types are not ruled out. I am looking at an *aspect* of the beliefs we hold— specifically, the intensity with which we believe. To reiterate: A pitfall of our pluralistic culture is the fading of our beliefs. The conversion that concerns me has been described by the Faith and Order Commission of the World Council of Churches as "Change from dead or nominal belief to a vibrant personal faith."[11] William James classically and cogently defined this conversion.

James sketches consciousness as composed of different groups and systems of belief that can exist relatively independent of each other. Each belief awakens a certain kind of interested excitement and gathers around itself a group of subordinate beliefs. He describes this situation:

There are dead feelings, dead ideas and cold beliefs, and there are hot and live ones; and when one grows hot and alive within us, everything has to re-crystallize about it.[12]

The temperature and location of our beliefs determine their life-shaping power. The hotter and more central they are, the more likely they are to design the way we are in the world:

It makes a great difference whether one set of ideas, or another, be the center of energy; and it makes a great difference, as regards any set of ideas which one may possess, whether they become central or remain peripheral.[13]

More to the point of this chapter, James calls the kind of change that occurs when cold beliefs become hot and central, conversion:

To say that one is "converted" means, in these terms [heat and location] that religious ideas, previously peripheral in the consciousness, now take a central place, and that religious aims form the center of one's energy.[14]

James incorporates case studies of this conversion in *The Varieties of Religious Experience.* Similar studies are as close as the nearest video store or newspaper stand. Rent, for example, the classic film *It's a Wonderful Life*, which fictionalizes such a conversion. George Bailey's beliefs in the value of his life and relationships are drained to the point of despair. An "angel" then portrays his family and town as if George had never existed, revitalizing faith in his own worth and trust in his relationships.

Molly Rush's story is not fiction.[15] Believing that the nuclear buildup in the United States put it on a deadly course, she supported demonstrations against the bomb. Fear of being arrested and having to leave her husband and, especially, her six children prevented her from taking part in any of these demonstrations. To the entreaties of the Berrigan brothers to become more active, she repeatedly asked, "What about the children?" At some point, Rush heard that question as a resolution to her dilemma. A newly fired conviction enabled her to practice civil disobedience for which she was indicted, convicted, and imprisoned.

These examples reflect similar stories in scripture. Circumstances and the arguments of his friends wear away at Job's belief in God's justice. Then, in the depths of his consternation, an experience of God overwhelms him. "Then the Lord answered Job out of the whirlwind" (Job 38:1 and 40:6). But Job's questions are silenced, not answered. His belief is recentered and made more vivid. "I had heard of you by the hearing of the ear, but now my eyes see you."

In the Christian Scriptures, fire and heat frequently symbolize the conversion of intensification.[16] John the Baptist distinguishes himself from the Christ: "He will baptize you with the Holy Spirit and *fire*." At Pentecost, "tongues as of fire" visibly signify a new empowerment, a change from fearful, dispirited people to prophets capable of birthing a church. But it is the detailed account of the couple returning to Emmaus from Jerusalem that is a paradigm of this conversion. The couple realize they have been converted as they say to each other, "Were not our hearts burning within us . . . ?" (Luke 24:32). We find in this story the pattern of all conversions. I will demonstrate that this pattern can be found in all significant experience.

THE PATTERNS OF CONVERSION

Whether the conversion is vertical (a change in the structure or the way we believe) or horizontal (a change in the contents or what we believe) or the kind of conversion I am describing (a change in the ardor with which we believe), the pattern according to which the change takes place seems the same. This pattern is illustrated in the work of those who use the significant, but common, human experiences of knowing, teaching, loving, dying, and being born as analogues of religious conversion. Choosing these events through which to track the pattern reinforces what I believe to be the thoroughly human character of conversion.

Knowing as Conversion

James Loder explicitly describes the activity of coming to know as an analogue of religious conversion. For him, all knowing is a "transforming event." The process he traces applies to solving puzzles *and* to Saul's recognition of the Christ on the road to Damascus.

Loder works out of a theory of knowing like the one outlined in the last chapter. Knowing is a constructive activity energized by the imagination, shaped in large part by our nature and nurture. The "transforming" element in the "event" is the conviction that we are justified in believing we have grasped an aspect of reality.

The process begins with *conflict;* disequilibrium is introduced into our environment. The lights going out in our home might trigger the process. A puzzle is set up— a trivial one, granted. But, as Loder remarks, regardless of how minor the disequilibrium is, there is the tendency to move towards equilibrium. On the other hand, "one cannot know what one does not care about . . . and the more one cares about the conflict, the more powerful will be the knowing event."[17]

The process continues with an *interlude for scanning* an "indwelling the conflicted situation with empathy for the problem and its parts."[18] Has a fuse died? Has a cable been cut? Has there been another continental-wide blackout? Interestingly, he places diversion at the heart of this scanning moment. The diversion may be as brief as the time it takes to look out the window.

Then there is a *constructive act of imagination.* An insight or solution presents itself. "Of course, I forgot to reset the timer on the lights!" The fourth step has two aspects. First, a *release* of the energy bound up in attending to the conflict, and second, an *opening* of the knower to himself or herself. Loder means that there is simultaneously a sense of relief and a new capacity to be conscious of one's self typically characterized by an expression such as "Now that is off my mind."[19]

Finally, there is *interpretation,* the step during which we work at incorporating the new knowledge into our living. We check the timer for vindication of the constructive act of imagination. And we reset it.

Teaching as Conversion

Maria Harris does not explicitly refer to the steps central to the teaching event as applicable to religious conversions, but the implication is there throughout. It registers in her conviction that the teaching act issues in recreation: the re-creation of the teacher, the subject matter, the students as subjects who matter, and the environment. Moreover, she easily moves back and forth between the language of educational theory, aesthetics, and religion. The title of her seminal work in this area indicates the connections she explores: *Teaching and Religious Imagination: An Essay in the Theology of Teaching.*

When Harris refers to the steps of the teaching act, she does not mean steps as in a ladder or even as on a walk, but steps as in a dance "where movement is both backward and forward, around and through, and where turns, returns, rhythm, and movement are essential."[20] *Contemplation* is the first step. For Harris, a teacher should begin by being still even before preparing the material to be taught. In that stillness, that stopping, that taking time, a teacher facilitates "the wide-awakeness necessary to 'take in' the personhoods involved,"[21] the subject that should matter, and the environment in which the teaching will take place.

Harris uses work with clay to illustrate *engagement*, the second step, and *form-giving*, the third step. In engagement, teachers move from the stillness to involvement as "sculptors move from feeling, touching, testing, learning about and contemplating clay to the moment of getting their hands and fingers involved in it."[22] Here Harris uses her experience in a class at Union Theological Seminary in New York City. Each student was blindfolded and then given a handful of clay. The teacher gave the following instructions:

> A form exists within the ball of clay you are holding in your hands and you are to find the form. But, you are to find it in the interchange with the clay; you are not to impose some prior vision of what is there. So, take the time, concentrate, discover that a form is taking shape. You will be able to feel it, to sense it, to intuit it. Once that happens, you can take off the blindfold and work from there.[23]

Her fourth step, *emergence*, could as readily be called *form-getting* and occurs at the moment when we discover the shape forming at our fingertips. Harris likens the moment to birth with all the tenuousness of neonatal existence. Yet, her fifth step, *release*, counsels against an overworking of the material. There is the tendency to put in one more crease, one more line. We must learn to let go—of clay, of students, of the subject that matters. I am sure that Harris would subscribe to the insight of the poet Paul Valery: A poem is never completed; at some point it is abandoned. This moment is analogous to the first step, contemplation, and in fact prepares us to enter that step once again. For Harris, the fifth step is not the final step, but the end of the set, which we simply begin again to continue the dance.

Love as Conversion

For over two decades, Rosemary Haughton has been exploring the commonplace of falling in love as a metaphor *as well as an experience* of religious conversion. The process begins with *remote preparation*, a wistfulness, a vague yearning for something like the experience of falling in love. Then there is *immediate preparation*, which creates a "weak spot."

To illustrate the process, Haughton repeatedly refers to the image of a stream that becomes dammed. A lake is formed in which flora and fauna can flourish. But when the water level rises or the damming elements are dislodged, the water will begin to flow with much greater force than in the original stream. The energy this breakthrough creates can be used to create other kinds of power—to pump, to drive engines, to light a town.[24] The "weak spot" she refers to in the stage of immediate preparation is an allusion to this analogy. It is the dislodging of normal expectations and settled attitudes. The next step, as we might expect, is *breakthrough* with all the terror and possibilities implied in her analogy.

She provocatively names the activity that makes breakthrough effective *the creation or re-creation of language*. The breakthrough cannot be private if it is to bear any fruit. A community with a shared language must sustain it, give it a plausibility structure, if you will. In an earlier work, *The Transformation of Man*, Haughton had been more specific. "If passion is a word for the breakthrough of power that makes true decision possible, marriage is the word for the 'language' in which and only in which the decision can be understood and worked out."[25] For her, marriage is the primary community within which the conversion of falling in love can be sustained.

Dying as Conversion

Elizabeth Kübler-Ross's stages of dying and grieving are well known.[26] Her descriptions have undoubtedly become classic because they have accumulated credibility. People can see their experience illustrated and illuminated by her descriptions. At no point does she equate the process she outlines with conversion as such. Yet, how much more significant could a change be than one from "people die—other people" to "I am dying and it is all right"? Denial, anger, bargaining, and depression mark the movement towards acceptance of a new way of being alive in the world.

Conversion has explicitly been called a kind of dying to self. In fact, Jacques Pasquier, a theologian and pastoral counselor, uses Kübler-Ross's outline of the stages to illustrate the process of religious conversion. He equates the stage of *denial* with resistance to some profound sense of dissatisfaction we feel as a result of crisis. *Anger* accompanies the "Why me?" as we sense that dying is part of the process of any spiritual journey. In *bargaining*, Pasquier says that we dialogue with a God reduced to our own image. "We sit at the same table to see how many compromises we can find: 'If you will give me this . . . I will give you that.'"[27]

As we realize that God is not a God to bargain with, we are flooded with a sense of our brokenness, our finitude. We experience helplessness (Kübler-Ross's *depression*). Then *maybe* we are ready for the act of acceptance—an activity Pasquier describes as surrender. But, as we might expect, acceptance of death is, for Pasquier, in this context of conversion, actually the choice for a new life.

Birth as Conversion

In her book, *Listening to Our Bodies: The Rebirth of Feminine Wisdom*, Stephanie Demetrakopoulos sees the birth process as a reflection and experience of a fundamental creative pattern in the universe. Being born and, for women, giving birth involves a pattern that serves as an analogue for all extremely intense experiences. She bases her description of this process and its implications on the experiments of Stanislav Grof.

Grof, who teaches psychiatry at Johns Hopkins, has for some years been using a variety of techniques to induce a reexperience of a person's birth. Demetrakopoulos summarizes his findings: "The patients experience the four stages of birth—*oceanic unity* with the mother, *entrapment in the birth canal* as labor begins, the *actual birth,* and the sense of a new kind of *universal bliss* after birth." [28]

The metaphor of birth has often been used to describe the particular kind of conversion I am concentrating on, that is, conversion within or more deeply into our religious belief. William James uses the terms *once-born* and *twice-born* as central categories in his famous work on religious experience. More recently, the expression "Born-again" has had a revival in Protestant evangelical groups as well as in charismatic groups among both Protestants and Catholics. There is little novelty, therefore, in equating the birth process to the process of conversion. Demetrakopoulos's unique contribution is that she sees the pattern of birth traced in every peak experience. We have been about tracing the pattern of conversion in those experiences—including birth. It remains to lift up that pattern.

The Shared Pattern

Not everyone whose work I have cited has the same number of moments or has them in the same order. But a similar pattern is easily discernible among them. Before the process begins, there is a period of equilibrium, a going along with no particular problem on the horizon—the intrauterine state as Grof names it. Then something happens. Conflict, engagement, the creation of a "weak spot," a diagnosis of terminal illness that triggers denial, anger, and bargaining, the struggle in the birth canal. Those who characterize the next two steps describe them as a kind of interlude, perhaps even a giving up of the conflict as in Kübler-Ross' designation of the step as depression. In some cases this may be followed by the construction of a resolution to the conflict (Loder) or by beginning to give form to it (Harris).

There is consensus concerning the critical moment of conversion, however, and almost identical language used to describe it: release, emergence, breakthrough, acceptance, birth.

Is it within *our* power to bring off these moments for ourselves or for each other? Or is religious conversion, of whatever kind, attributable only to God? Because, if God alone causes conversion, there is nothing more to say on the subject except perhaps to counsel prayer for renewed belief.

God's Role in Conversion

When the Soviet cosmonauts announced that they had searched the heavens, but had not bumped into God, many laughed at their childlike notion of God and heaven. We long ago abandoned the so-called three-tier universe of heaven above and hell below and the earth between. But it is a funny thing about the way images operate in our behavior, even when we know better. For example, is there anyone who still subscribes to the Ptolemaic universe, that is, a fixed earth around which the sun moves? Yet even the *New York Times*, that world-class chronicler of reality each day, publishes the times of the sun's rising and setting! Our behavior frequently betrays our better knowing. We may find ourselves raising our eyes to the heavens when referring to God or looking past our feet if we have occasion to mention hell. We are inclined to speak of the Deity or to the Deity as if God were one object among others in the universe. As if there were chairs and trees and people and God. Yet, to the question "Where is God?" most of us would answer, "Everywhere."

Ingrained images are hard to slough off, whether we know better or not. Consider the difficulty even people who believe God is neither male nor female have with abandoning the sole use of masculine pronouns to refer to Her. When we ask, therefore, what is God's role in conversion, preconscious images may dictate what we are able to hear in any answer offered. A further complication in any discussion of God or God's role in conversion is the realization that nothing we say is adequate to the subject. The best we can probably do is sketch models that are less and less inadequate. The God that can be captured in our concepts, cannot be a God worthy of worship. Yet we must speculate. We are a speculating species. The trick is to recognize that if no knowledge can claim point-for-point correspondence to the reality being plotted, how much more so must that lack of certainty be the case in any speculation about God. In *Models of God*, Sally McFague speaks to the issue succinctly:

> There are only versions, hypotheses, or models of reality (or God): the most that one can say of any construct, then, is that it is illuminating, fruitful, can deal with anomalies, has relatively comprehensive explanatory ability, is relatively consistent, has humane consequences, etc.[29]

Having said all this, let me propose that God has no specific role in conversion as God has no specific role in the cause of anything. God does not interfere in nature because God saturates all of reality. There is no need to interfere. Let me propose that a fruitful model of God's presence to the universe is as *Sheer In-ness and Of-ness* of whatever is.

GOD AS SHEER "IN-NESS" AND "OF-NESS"

The theologian Dietrich Bonhoeffer called our attention to the fact that God was being pushed more and more to the periphery of life. He echoes Laplace's response to Napoleon. "God as a working hypothesis in morals, politics, or science, has been surmounted and abolished; and the same thing has happened in philosophy and religion."[30] Earlier he had written:

> Religious people speak of God when human knowledge (perhaps simply because they are too

lazy to think) has come to an end, or when human resources fail—in fact it is always the *deus ex machina* that they bring to the scene, either for the apparent solution of insoluble problems, or as strength in human failure—always, that is to say, exploiting human weakness and human boundaries. Of necessity, that can go on only until people can by their own strength push these boundaries somewhat further out, so that God becomes superfluous as a *deus ex machina*. . . . It always seems to me that we are trying anxiously in this way to preserve some space for God; I should like to speak of God not on the boundaries but at the centre, not in weakness but in strength.[31]

What he speaks to, of course, is our penchant for reserving dependence on God for the gaps in our knowledge and power. When smallpox was a plague that could wipe out a city, people stormed heaven to be delivered from this evil. If they were delivered, they thanked God passionately. Now a serum has delivered the world from this malady. We no longer need God to fill this gap in our life. God is, as Bonhoeffer says, being pushed more and more to the periphery.

In the light of this situation, two possibilities present themselves. Either we continue to believe in the God of the Gaps, particularly as this God fills the gaps and needs in our own lives. This position privatizes religion even further than pluralism. Our faith is in nuclear weapons for our defense. Our faith is in God for our love life and our personal salvation.

The alternative that Bonhoeffer, among others, offers is the faith that God is not super nature, above and outside the world. Rather, "God is the beyond in our midst,"[32] "the Ground of our being,"[33] the Is-ing of whatever is.

Scientists have convinced most of us that we do not have relationships; we *are* our relationships. Whatever is, is, to the extent that it is, a tissue of relationships. As one philosopher phrased it, "To be is to be with."[34] But the superlative degree of *with* is *in* and *of*. We are most *with* what we are *in* and *of*. The spectrum of being seems to be marked off by the degree in which something can be in and of its environment. A rock, for example, exists in a minimal sense, restricted as it is in its capacity to be in and of its environment. A seed is another matter.

A companion question to that about the tree falling in the forest could be "If you plant a watermelon seed and return in due season to collect the fruit, where have the rind and pulp and new seeds come from?" Not the seed. The watermelon is transformed soil, air, rainwater, and fertilizer. The seed is the principle according to which these elements are organized into this watermelon. Living matter, therefore, has a substantially greater capacity than rocks to be in and of. That capacity is still limited, however, by the inability of three-dimensional "stuff" to occupy the same place at the same time. Persons are significantly less limited.

Person reality seems to be specified by an almost infinite capacity to be in and of other persons. It is the actualization of the capacity that creates a person. No better example exists of the dramatic emergence of personhood than the moment recorded in Helen Keller's

My Life when she was able to be in and of her teacher, Ann Sullivan Macy:

> Someone was drawing water and my teacher placed my hand under the spout. As the cool stream gushed over one hand she spelled into the other the word *water*, first slowly, then rapidly. I stood still, my whole attention fixed upon the motion of her fingers. Suddenly, I felt a misty consciousness as of something forgotten—a thrill of returning thought: and somehow the mystery of language was revealed to me. I knew then that w-a-t-e-r meant the wonderful cool something that was flowing over my hand. That living word awakened my soul, gave it light, hope, joy, set it free! There were barriers still, it is true, but barriers that could in time be swept away.[35]

Compenetration is possible in this instance through the gift of language.

My point is that if existence is commensurate with the capacity to be in and of, then a fruitful way of imaging God might be as *sheer in-ness and of-ness*.[36] Thomas Aquinas, the medieval philosopher and theologian, suggested such a model in his discussion of the presence of God:

> As the sun is present to lighted air, so long as it is lighted, so long is God present to whatever is, so long as it is. But be-ing [or is-ing] is innermost in each thing and most fundamentally present within all things. . . . Hence it must be that God is in all things, and innermostly.[37]

Aquinas seems to be saying that the most dramatic aspect of anything that is *is that it is* or (to freely translate his notion of *esse*) that it is-es. But the is-ing of anything is the God-ing of it. God is sheer in and of. Surely this is Augustine's point, too, when he says, "God is more me than I am myself."[38] It is *not* the position of the pantheist who identifies everything that exists as God with nothing left over.[39] Rather, it is the position of those who maintain that God is in and of the world (immanence), but God is more than in and of the world (transcendence). The relationship of persons to their body is sometimes used to illustrate this model. "The self is to the body as God is to the world" is a proportion frequently used to illustrate the In-ness and Of-ness of God.[40] Our penetration of the body is the condition of the body's existence. Yet, we are more than our bodies.

If God is in the tissues of the universe as the Depth of the universe, then all causality is drenched with Deity. God is not alongside other "natural" causes or "interfering" in nature either; God is in and of all elements that contribute to an event. This position puts a divine burden on us all. No one is excused from the prophetic vocation to make God's presence to the world evident in working for shalom. This position also puts a new spin on the means-end debate. Means must be as carefully selected as ends because in our means we "use" God. Whereas unworthy means may have been considered immoral, in this position, they must also be regarded as sacrilegious.

Are we then the means by which we convert ourselves? Do we "use" the "God who is more us than we are ourselves" to achieve our own conversion? Not quite.

OUR ROLE IN CONVERSIONS

The analogies of conversion that I have outlined strongly suggest that conversion is something that happens to us. We do not convert (at least not in the sense that I am using the term); we *are* converted. Yet, we contribute to the conversion experience. Perhaps, the old scholastic axiom "Grace builds on nature"[41] can help us understand our role in conversion in a way that is compatible with God's presence in and of all reality.

Grace literally means gift, and we frequently have the experience of events that occur in our life as "gift." Such everyday moments as understanding are typical of the experience of gift. We cannot make ourselves understand. We can work at achieving insight, but when and if it comes, it comes as gift. The so-called "Ah Ha!" moment is not within our control. We can study, but learning is gift, grace.

There seems to be a direct but not a necessary connection between effort and accomplishment. If the connection were a necessary one, practice could insure an inspired performance on the concert stage as well as the athletic field. But there is no such insurance. Our very designation of a performance as "inspired" suggests the grace quality I am talking about. Performers sometimes speak of the feeling of transcending themselves, of being "carried away" during such performances.

Nature is the effort, our efforts, our working on a problem or project that can be crowned by the grace of resolution or achievement—but not necessarily so. The patterns of conversion that we studied in the last chapter have these elements of effort, struggle, and strain. But the moment of conversion "happens" more or less gracefully.

The solution to the lights failing *dawns*. The form *emerges* from the clay. Love *breaks through*. At some moment acceptance of our death *occurs*. We *are* born or reborn. However, the fact that we cannot commandeer grace does not mean that we cannot expend effort towards conversion.

Recall Corita Kent's remarks about the gift of celebration: "If you ice a cake, light sparklers and sing, something celebrative *may* happen."[42] In the next chapter, I will look at equivalents of icing a cake, lighting sparklers, and singing in the context of conversion. The two moments where we seem to have entry into the process of conversion, where we can exert effort, where nature can anticipate grace are the first and second moments: the contemplative moment and the moment of conflict.

※

CHAPTER FOUR

PRECIPITATING CONVERSION

The prospect haunts me that someone may have read the previous chapter as an exhortation to heat up our beliefs regardless of what we believe. I am troubled that someone may hear in my words echoes of President Eisenhower who opined that our government makes no sense "unless it is founded in a deeply felt faith—and I don't care what it is."[1] I do care; it does make a difference what we believe. Whatever is said in this chapter, therefore, must be played against the rejection of relativism and the criteria offered to evaluate beliefs described earlier.

In that context we will look more closely at belief and the affect that vitalizes our faithing. Then we will study those moments of the conversion process to which we have access, namely, contemplation and conflict. Not that we can convert ourselves, but we can contemplate and take advantage of conflict or put ourselves in its way, and conversion *may* happen.

BELIEF

We are interested in the kind of conversion in which "cold beliefs" become "hot"; in which "dead or nominal beliefs" become "vibrant and personal." We are, therefore, first of all, interested in belief. I have already described a belief as an interpretation of reality, which, when it is justified, goes by the name "knowledge." Here I wish to note that our beliefs function as judgments about reality and as conditions of experience; they cluster around core beliefs, and our actual beliefs are often different from the beliefs we profess.

The Function of Beliefs

As Judgments about Reality

Every declarative sentence constitutes a judgment and a belief. Test that thesis. Read a paragraph about anything. Insert before each declarative sentence the phrase "I believe." For instance, insert the phrase before the sentences of this section. ("I believe we are interested in the kind of conversion. . . ." "I believe we are first of all. . . .") It makes sense until you come to the sentences that are instructions such as "Test that judgment. . . ." "I believe test that judgment" is nonsensical. But declarative sentences are well named. They verbalize—declare something about reality that we judge to be real, to be the case, to be so. It is raining. I love you. Joey is boring.

We do not usually think of ourselves as reciting a credo when we string together a series of declarative sentences. And we are not—at least not in our times. But, as knowing at one time included a carnal note,[2] so belief had an equally full-blooded history. *Believe* comes from the same Indo-European root (*leubh*) that gives us love *and* lust. It is also possible to see some of these elements in the Latin *credo*, which is usually translated as "I believe." The "cre" of *credo* is a variant of *cor* or heart as in our cognates *cordial* and *accord*. The "do" is the verb to put or place from which we derive our words *do* and *donation*. A more vigorous rendering therefore of "I believe" is "I set my heart."[3]

We still use erotic expressions around our discussion of beliefs. We hold some beliefs dear, cling to them, cherish them People are described as wedded to a belief.[4] The emotional investment, however, is not usually in the belief itself, but rather in the reality mediated by the belief or the experience promised by the belief.

Coming to believe that my spouse is unfaithful could be an extremely painful and long-resisted judgment. The belief that my spouse is faithful may be a comforting belief that I cling to and cherish. But it is the faithful spouse him or herself, *the reality about which I believe,* that dominates our attention and affection.

As the Condition of Experience

Beliefs also function as thresholds *to* experience. I believe this is the college I should go to, the job I should take, the person I should marry. Believing in these cases is the condition of experiencing the reality. Were I to disbelieve any of these judgments, I close off the life the belief offers. These are the kinds of beliefs of which it was written, "I believe in order that I may understand."[5] Or, as I have suggested, "I believe in order that I may experience." It stands to reason that I am propelled into the experience with a power in direct proportion to the gusto with which I believe. If I am positive that this is the college for me (technically impossible of course, since I have yet to attend the school), I am more likely not only to attend the school, but also to seek out and relish those aspects of the place that validate my belief.

Core Beliefs

Not all beliefs are created equal.[6] Our beliefs seem to cluster around key convictions that account for and shape the beliefs gathered around them. Paul Pruyser tells the story of speaking to a fellow panelist on the role of women in society. In Pruyser's words, this panelist:

> held forth on the virtues of the married state and the satisfactions of motherhood. Hers was a very traditional viewpoint, and she buttressed it by frequent citations of Bible verses and assertions that this traditional view was sacred, since it was ordained by God.[7]

When Pruyser suggested that roles of women and men in the Christian Scriptures more likely reflected the Hellenistic culture of the time, she shifted the discussion to the inerrancy of scripture. As she realized that Pruyser did not share that belief, she tried to cut off the conversation. Pruyser concluded, "Belief in the inerrancy of scripture was apparently her key belief, and it seemed even higher than her belief in God—all other beliefs depended upon it."[8]

Operative and Professed Belief Systems

Surely the woman in that story would profess that God's existence and love for the world was her key belief, but according to Pruyser, her speech betrayed her. The discrepancy between what we profess and how we operate is sometimes described as the discrepancy between theory and practice, sometimes labeled hypocrisy. It is hypocrisy if there is conscious deviation from what we claim to believe and what our actions indicate we do in fact believe. But often the discrepancy is not conscious. In any case, making our operative beliefs conform to our professed beliefs has long been thought of as a kind of conversion to which everyone is called.

Religious Beliefs

Religious beliefs by definition (*religion* means binding) should be those beliefs on which "we place our heart," to which we are totally committed. Yet these beliefs have the same characteristics as other beliefs. Religious beliefs, like other beliefs of their kind, may be treasured in themselves, for the comfort, the joy, the energy such judgments provide. But their larger meaning is the reality they make accessible to us: the experience of a loving, provident Deity, the divinity of flesh, access to forgiveness, strength, and a community of saints, to cite just some of the judgments found in Christian creeds.

While they are judgments about reality, they are also the condition of experience. To believe in God is the price of experiencing God. It is possible that a nonbeliever would experience God, of course, as it is possible I could be happily surprised in a job I had initially believed was not suitable. Possible perhaps, but not probable. A closer analogue would be the judgment that this person should not be my spouse. That belief shuts off all possibility of being corrected by experience, because it cuts off the experience.

The dual nature of belief as judgment and the condition of experience is captured in the exclamation "Amen" not as it perfunctorily closes perfunctory prayers, but as it is ardently shouted during particular preaching situations. *Amen* means "It is so!" and "Let it be so!" Simultaneously a judgment about reality and a hope for the experience (or continued experience) of the reality.

A way of referring to the kind of conversion about which I am speaking in this section might be to talk of heating up our Amens! How can we reinvigorate our believing, reintroduce some of those lustful and longing elements into our credo? We must look at affect or emotion.

AFFECT

Unfortunately, considering the central role that affect plays in human existence, there is little consensus on exactly what is covered by the word. Feelings and emotions, surely. But are feelings and emotions interchangeable? Most psychologists would say no.

Feelings seem to be those interior sensations of attraction or repulsion that flavor everything we experience. According to the most prominent school of psychologists today, emotions are appraisals of situations that are frequently accompanied by feelings but not necessarily so.[9] We evaluate the flavored composition that our imagination proposes as reality and simultan-eously respond organically. I sense that I have been slighted and I become angry. I see a bear and I become frightened.

One of the major issues that divide the students of emotion is whether there is one basic sense of bodily dis-ease that we experience differently according to the situation in which we find ourselves. In one case, we experience it as anger; in another, as fear—depending on the context.[10] Most psychologists, however, think that the various emotions are physiologically distinguishable.

Another issue more relevant to our discussion concerns the role of our will in the experience of emotions. Do we *choose* to be angry? Do we *choose* to be in love? Robert C. Solomon is one philosopher who appears to answer that question with an unequivocal yes. In two intriguingly written books, he has argued:

> We do not "fall in" love at all. Quite to the contrary, the fall is rather a creation, which we have been taught to make by a thousand movies, stories and novels; its most essential ingredient— too often hidden in the language of "spontaneous" and "chance"—is personal *choice*.[11]

On closer analysis, however, even Solomon qualifies his notion of choice such that it resembles the nature-gift situation that I described above. In fact, his decision to see emotions as decisions rather than gifts seems rather to reflect a choice of his own. We see this when he speaks of falling out of love. As he comments sympathetically on the agony of those whose love is ill-advised or unrequited, he recognizes that their experience seems to give lie to the choice factor in love—and in all emotions. Certainly, if it were within one's power, one would simply choose out of such a painful situation. He sticks to his decision, however, and chalks up the seeming inability to choose out of love to an *unwillingness* to do so because one's self is at stake. In a revealing comment that follows, the source of his decision is unmasked:

> Again, the difference between "cannot" and "will not" is not always clear, particularly in the realm of emotions. But as a historical corrective to the emphasis on passivity, at least, our own emphasis should be on the latter.[12]

We will find this emphasis helpful in the context of commitment. At this point we can agree with Solomon that emotions are not just passions in the sense that we undergo them. They require thought on our part, the so-called cognitive dimension involved in appraising the situation: This person is lovable; this situation is embarrassing.

Emotions then are passionate responses to the appraisal of a situation, responses that urge us to action. Emotions are moving in two ways: They move us in the sense of producing a detectable physiological change in our bodies, and they move us to express some behavior appropriate to the emotion. We interpret the situation ahead to be a bear on the path. We evaluate that as dangerous. Simultaneously, our body registers the fear in sweaty palms, increased heart beat, butterflies in the stomach, and perhaps weakness in the knees. With equal simultaneity, we experience the urge to run.

Corrections of our original interpretation can increase or lower the intensity of the emotion. Judging that the bear is bearing down on me can produce terror. Spying a chain around the bear's neck, obviously tied to something sturdy, can mitigate the fear to manageable proportions. In other words, emotions are amenable to reason. That is, they can be diffused (or reheated) by subsequent analyses. I could be persuaded, for example, that the bear I was so frightened about was actually a man in a raccoon coat. But the appeal is never purely cerebral. The logic must engage us on the feeling level. Of course, the prospect of a bear on our trail might make an alternative possibility intrinsically attractive.

Emotions run the gamut of intensity. But, they are rarely as "pure" as the fear I have just described. I might be jealous of a friend's good fortune and at the same time embarrassed to be harboring that jealousy. In addition, I might be angry with myself for being embarrassed at an emotion that appears to have occurred spontaneously.

My point here is to recall the inevitable cognitive-affective dimension (body-mindedness) of all our activity, and also to underline the realization that it is the affective dimension that moves us. Not only does love make the world go around, affect makes everything go.[13] Paradoxically, as we stop to contemplate, one of the things we will be looking for or at is what moves us.

CONTEMPLATION

In the patterns of conversion outlined in the last chapter, a moment of stillness marked almost every process. That moment sometimes followed, sometimes preceded conflict, but in any case, stillness seems essential to conversion. Unfortunately, the pace and distractions of modernity make the need for a deliberate scheduling of the contemplative moment both more urgent and more difficult to do. A famous experiment reinforces the effect of pace on our beliefs.[14]

A few years ago, a number of seminarians at the Divinity School in Princeton University were given the task of preparing a sermon on the text of the Good Samaritan. The Good Samaritan, of course, was that figure in the Christian Scriptures who, unlike those who preceded him on the same trip, had picked up a man who had been attacked by robbers and left for dead. Not only did the Samaritan pick him up, but he "bandaged his wounds, having poured oil and wine on them. Then he put him on his own animal, brought him to an inn, and took care of him" (Luke 10:34). Then the next day he gave the innkeeper money to continue caring for the victim. Moreover, the Samaritan promised to reimburse the innkeeper for any additional expenditures incurred in attending the man who had been attacked.

After preparing the sermons, the seminarians were told, under various conditions, to proceed to another building to deliver them. What was being tested, however, was not their sermon preparation or delivery. It was their response to a derelict-like figure that had been planted on the path to the other building. We might expect that the seminarians, preparing as they were for a life in ministry and most recently having immersed themselves in this great story of charity, would take the Samaritan as their model; that they would look after the apparently unfortunate person on their path. And many did. But, many did not.

The principal variable between those who attended to the person at their feet and those who did not was the amount of time that had been allotted by the professor for getting to the building where the sermon was to be delivered. Those who had to hurry the most were least likely even to see the "derelict." The pace of modernity can have that effect. It can subvert our most dearly held ideals, blindside us from our visions. Hurry is a major distraction from the business of being about our business.

If the pace of modernity is distracting, the complexity of modernity can tempt us to seek distraction, tempt us to thoughtlessness. Socrates' warning that the unexamined life is not worth living can go unheeded in a world whose complexity can paralyze our thought processes. The very technology that makes us exquisitely aware of this complexity also puts at our disposal the distractions that can contribute to a thoughtless existence by making the complications unnoticeable. At this writing more than half the homes in the United States have VCRs. Almost as many have cable connections for their television. A glut of viewing possibilities is available to us every hour of every day. But television programmers are aware, and Neilson numbers confirm, that given the choice, most of us will choose to watch situation comedies whose plots turn on homely and manageable problems. The documentaries, dealing with systemic issues that seem to defy resolution, go begging for audiences.

A distracting existence that suffices for some of us is a luxury not allowed many others on the planet. Whereas, in too many places, including our own country, peoples' psychic energy is drained in the effort to survive, to endure, our energies are diffused, not drained. As the philosopher Robert Johann put it, we do not want with a passion.[15] Our desires are not focused. Our beliefs are weak and fragmentary. Surely, the refocusing and "heating up" of our beliefs in a profound and worthy way is the conversion that so many religious traditions call for. And, if conversion is not something we can do for ourselves, we can at least put ourselves into the occasion of conversion. But not easily. Forewarning ourselves of some of the major difficulties we can encounter as we try to enter the contemplative mode may forearm us.

Post-Ignition Syndrome

Is there anyone who has not turned off a car's ignition only to have the motor grumble, rattle, and shake until it seems it will fall out of the front end? As I understand it, this phenomenon can be eliminated by slowing the timing of the carburetor. If our internal timing is too fast, attempts to turn off the ignition, to be still, will exhibit post-ignition symptoms. Our minds will be flooded with memories, urgent nudges to attend to other business, worries we thought we had dismissed.

Slow, deep breathing can help to stop the rattling. Soothing music can also have that effect. Short, pleading prayers can help. "Have mercy" is enough. In the worst-case scenario, where nothing seems to still the internal racket, simply waiting out the noise wins the time. In the post-ignition syndrome of our cars, the noise stops eventually and very few engines actually fall out of the chassis.

Fear

Becoming still can introduce another difficulty however. In the silence, we may find that we believe little to nothing, that our hearts are disengaged, that our credos echo hollowly in the quiet. In other words, the silence can become thunderous and threatening because of the emptiness that greets us. We can find ourselves longing for the familiarity of the post-ignition noise. We can be tempted to scrap altogether the effort to be still.

At this point, the effort must be committed to God. It is God's problem. We have disposed ourselves, we want to want to believe. "Help our unbelief." If we are graced with peace, so be it. If not—back to square one, but this time with greater conviction that we are waiting for God's gift. Being still, like understanding, like learning, like celebration, like anything that graces our existence, cannot be grabbed, achieved, or won. It is gift.

Fascination

Ironically, an additional difficulty can meet us even in the midst of the stillness, and that is a fascination with the stillness. Thomas Merton wrote in his journal that the contemplative experience was so intoxicatingly wonderful that he could envision someone ready to kill to recover the experience. Becoming overly enamored of the exercise of poking around our beliefs and relationships warrants the description, navel gazing.

At this point the value of a companion in the exercise becomes obvious. Called a soul friend, a guru, a spiritual director in the various traditions, such a companion on-the-way can call us back to the purpose of our contemplation: discernment.

DISCERNMENT

Discerning suggests a studied contemplation of the environment until nameable shapes emerge. Imaged in discernment is something of the sailor on night watch straining to spy obstacles to the journey or land for the journey's end. What are we looking at? What are we looking for?

If we are very still, the outlines of our worldview may emerge in the stillness. Then, as physicians palpitate the body to distinguish healthy and unhealthy spheres, we can feel among and through the body of our beliefs. Where do we wince? What beliefs are feverish with affect? What do we want to believe?

CONFLICT

The moment of dis-equilibrium, dis-ease, conflict, or struggle is central to all theories of conversion, all kinds of conversion, and all patterns of conversion. The moment can arise from the simple task of living, and it can be induced by ourselves and/or others. But the experience of conflict does not guarantee conversion, nor even resolution of the conflict.

The Centrality of Conflict

The kind of conversion one is talking about hardly matters. Movement through the developmental stages (vertical conversion) is triggered by a dis-equilibrating event of some sort. Erik Erikson, for example, saw young adulthood as the period in which persons typically become capable of intimacy, that is, the structures become available for advancement to the next stage. Confronted with a crisis such as falling in love, a person either enters a profound and lasting relationship or retreats to isolation.[16]

Change of content conversions (horizontal) are similarly triggered. "There are no atheists in foxholes." Whether such universality is valid is beside the point; the expression documents our experience that in crisis situations our belief system can change dramatically. The crisis need not be as threatening as residence in a foxhole to foster conversion however. "Engagement," "creation of a 'weak moment,'" "confrontation," "struggle"—the range of terms used to illuminate and illustrate conversion patterns in the previous chapter suggest the spectrum of disequilibrating events. Regardless of the severity of the dis-easing moment, the moment itself is indispensable.

James makes the same point with regard to the revitalization of belief. "Emotional occasions, especially violent ones, are extremely potent in precipitating mental rearrangements."[17] He includes hope and happiness among the "explosive" emotional occasions—a point that we may find surprising. But we should not.

An interesting stress questionnaire has been around for some time now.[18] It assigns a stress quotient to changes that life almost inevitably serves up to all of us.

As we might expect, the death of a spouse or a child leads the list. But, unexpectedly, a marriage and the birth of a child are almost as stressful. And switching to a better job is almost as stress-filled as being fired. The point seems to be that any significant change, even one that is anticipated as delightful, introduces conflict into our lives and can rearrange and revitalize our beliefs.

The Nature of Conflict

Walter E. Conn broadly defines conflict in the context of conversion as the struggle we experience when we find our personal theory of reality "inadequate to meet the complex reality of the natural, interpersonal, socially structured human world that is life."[19] Psychologists tell us that our personal theory has four basic functions: (1) to enable us to absorb and identify new data; (2) to maintain a favorable proportion of pleasure over pain for the long haul; (3) to foster self-esteem; and (4) to maintain the personal theory of reality as it is.[20]

1. We have a filing system of whose extent and organizational scheme we are mostly unaware. If something should appear to us as a spaceship hovering outside our window, but our file contains no such cubbyhole, a conflict is introduced. The conflict will not be resolved until we either begin to believe in alien life forms or find some other belief under which we can file this new data.

2. Unless we are masochists, a pathological condition, we constantly calculate the proportion of impending or existing pain to the pleasure it will garner. I embrace the pain of dieting anticipating the pleasure I believe I will experience as a healthy sylph. I believe that the long, painful hours that I put into my medical studies will issue in a pleasurably fruitful career as a physician. When our calculus cannot foresee any balance of pleasure, when the suffering appears to be senseless as in the death of a child or the physical pain of the terminally ill, we experience a crisis of exquisitely anguishing dimensions.

3. Few people have wonderful self-images. Yet, as poorly as we may esteem ourselves, whatever threatens the little esteem we have is conflicting. The sorrow that follows bad grades in school or an unsatisfactory evaluation at work is seldom about what we have not learned or our poor work habits; it is mostly about the threat to our self-worth.

4. Studies abound demonstrating that our beliefs will join forces, close ranks, circle the wagons as it were, to maintain our personal theory of reality. In other words, the last function of our theories of reality is to maintain themselves. As our bodies galvanize to expel a foreign body (against our will in the case of a kidney

transplant, for example), so our beliefs resist change in location and temperature when those changes threaten the status quo. Logic and evidence, the classic tools of persuasion, cannot of themselves break the ranks of our belief system. It is the belief system that dictates the appeal of logic and what shall be considered evidence. We find ourselves seeking persuasions that cater to our operating belief systems. Collecting examples of our vulnerability to aberrant resolutions of conflicts is something of a cottage industry among social scientists

MANIPULATING RESOLUTION TO CONFLICT

Over a generation ago, Leon Festinger, a sociologist, described the peculiar "logic" employed by smokers who believed that smoking is harmful: Smoking is so enjoyable, it is worth the risk. The individual can always beat the statistics. Not every risk to life and limb can be avoided. The weight gain that would probably result with the cessation of smoking would be equally health threatening.[21]

Another study led by Festinger, *When Prophecy Fails*,[22] describes a famous example of finding new "evidence." In the late 40s or early 50s a group assembled around the conviction that the world would be destroyed by a flood on December 21, but the band of believers would be rescued by a spaceship. Sociologists from the University of Minnesota infiltrated the group to record the fate of the believers' convictions if nothing happened on December 21. Nothing did happen, of course. And some of the members of the group abandoned the belief. The hard-core members, however, continued to believe. They rationalized the lack of a flood and the saving spaceship by saying that God had intervened to prevent the cataclysm. The pertinent information for our purpose is that prior to December 21 the group had been quite secretive about their beliefs, but after that day, they began to proselytize quite passionately.

A commentator summarized the significance of this change in strategy. "Since the only acceptable form of truth had been undercut by physical proof, there was but one way out of the corner for the group. They had to establish another type of proof for the validity of their beliefs: social proof."[23] In other words, if the most obvious evidence was disconfirming, other evidence would be sought by adding new members to the group. Extending their plausibility structures would confirm the plausibility of their convictions.

We may all be able to identify with a less extreme, more homely example of purchasing a car. Mechanical problems with the car or advertisements of the same auto less expensively priced are likely to produce rationalizations similar to those of the space cult.

We, too, are apt to find ourselves using a special "logic" and seeking "evidence" for the fact that we made a good choice, got a good buy. We tell ourselves, "The service is better at this dealer, therefore, the extra money was worth it; in fact, I will probably save money in the end." "This mechanical problem is a fluke; the car will be better than ever once this kink is worked out or adjusted." Not everyone will take this tack however, just as not everyone in the group above continued to believe.

These examples demonstrate how easily we are manipulated—by ourselves as well as others. Some advertising agencies make their living on this information. TV commercials during the Super Bowl cost almost a million dollars. Even at that price, the corporations line up to hawk their wares because "It pays to advertise." To keep it paying, advertisers cater to a generic version of our personal theories. Their messages are easily labeled and absorbed; they promise an end to all pain; they pander to our self-esteem.

Given this background, can we ever in a nonmanipulative way precipitate the conflict that may be the occasion of conversion?

TEACHING AND PREACHING: ACTIVITIES THAT PROMOTE CONFLICT

How do you feed lions? Very carefully. How do you promote conversion? Even more carefully. Introducing conflict into one's own or another's life is always risky business. Resolution is not guaranteed. As we saw in the last section, if and when it comes, the beliefs that are heated or moved to center stage are not necessarily those that enhance existence; they may be those beliefs that simply preserve existence or are even destructive of existence. Teaching and preaching are two activities that ideally promote conversion very carefully.

Dated images may flood our mind at the mention of teaching and preaching: the school teacher in front of a classroom of children, the preacher in a pulpit speaking to or at a congregation. But teaching is not confined to classrooms. In fact most of the teaching we experience is the teaching we do to ourselves; it is called learning. Similarly preaching is not a pulpit-only activity.

Teaching can also have aims other than the promotion of conflict toward conversion. The acquisition of a skill, clarification of a concept, and explanation of a procedure are frequently the featured aims of a teaching/learning session. But even when these are the articulated objectives, congeries of beliefs are being promoted. Implicit in the most apparently value-free teaching-learning situations (say, teaching-learning a multiplication table) are at least the beliefs that teaching and learning this times table is possible and desirable and that this is the way to do it.

Preaching usually includes a teaching dimension. Preaching may also aim at clarification and explanation. But it is more directly and frequently focused on conversion—and the conversion we are talking about: the change from dead or nominal belief to a vibrant faithing.

It is educational theory, however, in which some of our best clues for nonmanipulative conversion can be found. A team of educators has plotted a taxonomy of affect that I have adapted as the heat history of a belief.[24] A taxonomy is an ordered classification of anything according to an organizing principle. The educators classified the desired outcomes of learning in the affective domain. (What do we want this person, these persons, to experience as a result of this teaching-learning situation?) They organized the continuum according to the degree of interiorization, the degree to which the experience becomes more and more central to a person's identity. The educators focused on the behaviors by which the depth of affect can be recognized. The behaviors are receiving, responding, valuing, organization, and characterization.

In the middle of a made-for TV movie, a public service announcement calls attention to world hunger. For a moment I attend to the tragedy. That can be the end of it, of course. I can go about my business and not advert to that momentary awareness again. If I keep attending to the experience, I am courting the questions, the conflict, it arouses. If I then take steps to act on this recognition of the unequal distribution of goods, I am demonstrating that I value the insight. When I begin to organize my life around the insight into injustice, I have been converted. When this insight characterizes my life, I have been transformed.[25]

The taxonomy we have just traced suggests the moments of teaching or preaching activity that promote conversion. From the teacher's perspective these moments are proposing, stimulating, providing opportunities to exercise the belief, providing opportunities to critique the belief, ritualizing its characterizing quality. From the learner's perspective: noticing, pleasurable attending, acting on the belief, critiquing the belief, transformation. The teaching and learning activities may be distinct, but the person engaging in them need not be.

Proposing/Noticing

That "Stockholm is the capital of Sweden" may lie unnoticed among our beliefs until a trivia game calls it forth from our information bed or a travel agent puts it on our route through Scandinavia. In either case the attention required is negligible (trivia games) or short-lived (trip). "What I have and do not need belongs to those who need it" is a belief of another color. It may lie happily unnoticed just at the edge of our belief system. Attend to such a belief and the strains of dissonance will be sounded. Every belief invested in our lifestyle will work at distracting us from further attending.

Any belief is legitimately called radical when it strikes at the roots of our identity, entire belief system and lifestyle. To heat up any such belief and move it to the center stage is so disequilibrating that the fact that it ever happens makes conversion seem like a supernatural event—an interference in the laws of inertia. That it happens with persons as disparate as Che Gueverra and Mother Teresa suggests that "nature is wilder than we imagined, and more varied."

Stimulating/Pleasurable Attending
Speaking of the poem "Another Place," which concludes with the line "It becomes possible to think of going," Marilyn Ferguson says that new life begins not with action but with awareness. We are on our way "when it first becomes possible to think of going."[26] This is the moment during which the teacher stimulates and the learner entertains possibility. If decision enters into the conversion process at any point, this is the point. Here we determine whether to resolve the conflict prematurely by distracting ourselves from an unbidden and unwanted belief that has emerged in consciousness. If we continue to toy with the idea, to explore the belief, we are on the slippery slope to the birth canal. We are engaged. It is not for nothing that *engagement* refers both

to a period of covenanted courtship and a battle with enemy forces. We may find ourselves alternately angry, bargaining, and depressed.

Reinforcing/Exercising the Belief

If we find ourselves at this moment, we have been converted. We are taking the belief seriously, a criterion of conversion according to Berger and Luckmann.[27] If we expose ourselves willingly to conditions of the underclass that may reinforce our belief that possessions beyond our needs belong to others, we have begun to emerge, be born, experience a breakthrough, accept a death of sorts. We begin to live "Amen!" "It is so!" "Let it be so!"

Critiquing the Belief

Hitler's book *Mein Kampf* is as much a story of conversion as is Augustine's *Confessions*. Conversion is not intrinsically good; it is, in its simplest description, a mechanism for resolving conflict. We have seen that we are inclined to resolve dissonance in ways that will nourish our personal theory of reality. As dramatically as we need plausibility structures (a community who believes with us) in order to believe, we need critiquing structures (a community to help us evaluate our beliefs) to bring to bear the criteria outlined in Chapter Two.

As we continue to notice, nourish, exercise, and critique our beliefs, we can hope to be characterized by them. That involves conversion squared or transformation. That is what commitment is all about.

CHAPTER FIVE

❀

COMMITMENT

We make commitments all the time. "I'll meet you for lunch on Friday," we say, unaware of the God-like pronouncement we have just made. In making such a promise I simultaneously say that I can and will order my life, shape the future, *arrange reality* such that you can expect me to be at the table next week. Some thinkers see the capacity to promise as the defining note of personhood.[1] This feature, more than any other, seems to reflect our divine image. But in its exercise, we also bump into our creaturehood. Our commitment may not survive a car accident, an illness, a tardy airline, a faulty memory, or a conflicting commitment.

The promise to lunch together, a relatively trivial commitment, exemplifies the kinds of commitments we make all day, every day. "I'll call you back." "I'll get out that report." "I'll fix dinner." While the trustworthiness of such commitments eases our days and nights, in this chapter I am more interested in overarching commitments—those commitments to which we are devoted, the commitments that transform us, that account for who we are.

From these latter commitments and especially from commitments to persons, we can tease out the elements of commitment generally. In this chapter, I will look at the meaning of commitment, the difference it makes. I will then examine how appropriate these elements and meanings are when God is the subject of our commitment. I will also discuss how people committed to the Good News God "do" commitment. Because I consider the missionary vocation the best example of what Christians are called upon to do, I will explore in this section what evangelizing means. Finally, I will consider ways of nourishing this commitment.

The Elements of Commitment

When we commit ourselves, we give our word; we pledge ourselves; we plight our troth. To what? To the object of our commitment. To do what? To promote the existence of that to which we are committed. Whether we commit ourselves to a plan, a principle, a value, an institution, a profession or a person, what we have pledged is to order our life, shape the future, *arrange reality* such that the plan is implemented; the principle or value is increasingly cultivated, becomes more evident in our life and society; the profession is improved; the existence of the person is enhanced.

Beliefs cause, energize, and shape our commitments, but they are not the object of our commitment. Belief motivates our making a commitment. I believe I love this man and he loves me. Not only does this belief move me to commit myself to him "'til death do us part," but the belief nourishes the living out of my commitment; it describes for us and for others the nature of the commitment. Finally, it dictates the terms of the commitment, what I must do—the loving thing always. But my beliefs are not the object of my commitment, my beloved is—and is more properly called—the subject of my commitment.

Beliefs are like transistors that make hearing music possible for us. We may treasure the radio in the light of the realities it makes available to us, allowing us to possess what we hoped for. But to confuse the radio with what it makes available could preclude our trading in a particular radio for one that takes better advantage of electronic advances, one that enhances the quality of our access. Similarly, when we make our beliefs the subject of our commitment, they can preclude surprises from the reality they mediate—whether that reality is my friend, my lover, or my God.

The Meaning of Commitment

A lived commitment shapes and then transforms our lives. Commitment also contributes to the shape and transformation of the subject of our commitment. This is the meaning of commitment, the difference it makes.

Commitments provide the structures upon which we flesh out our lives. They dictate what time we will wake up, where we will spend our days, to whom we shall come home. They order what we will do at work and how we will do it. Sustained commitment transforms us.

As we live out commitment, we more and more take on the characteristics of the subject of that commitment. If we are committed to justice, as we continue to do just acts, we evolve into a just person. Justice is reflected in every relationship. What may have begun as isolated actions becomes a constant pattern through which we engage all of reality.

The subjects of our commitments are also transformed. In the case of justice, the subject may be transformed by being called into existence, by simply being where it had not been before. Or it may be transformed by becoming more evident or more entrenched or more creative in its application. But our discussion in this chapter is derived from commitments to persons and, particularly, from the mutual commitments between persons.[2] In these commitments we see the transforming power of lived commitment, not only in the form of our lives, but in the flesh. Consider the often uncanny resemblance to each other of longtime spouses. The resemblance is not so much in the bone and skin of their bodies as in the expressions on their faces, the similarity of their gestures, their choice of words, and their responses to situations. Similar mutual transformations occur between longtime friends. It seems as persons continue to like each other, they become like each other.

But these visible transformations barely reflect a more profound transformation taking place. New identities are emerging. The persons committed to each other are coming to *be* spouses and friends. The husbandly or wifely or friendly act becomes not simply second nature, but first nature. It becomes not only inconceivable but physically impossible to act in any other way. Our actions are now the inevitable effects of who we have become.

Yet, paradoxically, commitment frees us. When commitment becomes effortless, when it becomes impossible to do anything other than live out our commitment, it may seem that we have paid a price in freedom. Quite the opposite. But confusing free will and freedom can lead to that conclusion.

Thinking of free will as a power tool that enables us to shape ourselves resolves the confusion. When we commit ourselves to rising at dawn each day, as we hear the alarm those first mornings, we are very aware of the exercise of our will. The exertion may, in fact, be more than we can manage. But as we continue to live out our resolution, rising becomes easier and easier until we cannot sleep in. We no longer need to exercise our free will however. We are free in the richest sense of that term. We have become free because we are who we want to *be*—early risers.

Unfortunately, we rarely attain such an experience of freedom. Most of us can sympathize with Paul: "I do not do the good I want, but the evil I do not want is what I do" (Romans 7:19). Most of us experience too frequently the strain and drain of exercising our free will. Only a vivid commitment keeps us making those efforts.

COMMITMENT TO GOD

If we have been converted as described in the last chapter, if our beliefs have excited us to commitment, to whom are we committed? We Christians believe we are committed to One who was first committed to us, who has given us his Word, who has plighted to us her Troth and Way and Life. In the Christian tradition we are committed to the God revealed in our scriptures, codified in our creeds, and celebrated in our rites. A God, whom we believe, is Emmanuel, God with us.

Any uniqueness in our commitment to God is on God's part. For our part, we can commit ourselves only humanly, as we do in any commitment. But, we ask, can we bring the same expectations to this commitment? We know that God's love for us enhances our existence, transforms us. But, is it not hubris to talk of enhancing or transforming God?

It would be if our God were the "Unmoved Mover" of the Greeks, unchanging and unchangeable. But everything we have come to believe of this God through tradition and revelation speaks against an impassible God. In fact, we know that the divine love for us has already had a transforming effect on the Godhead. "God so loved the world that he gave his only Son . . . (John 3:16) who, though he was in the form of God . . . emptied himself, taking the form of a slave, being born in human likeness" (Philippians 2:6–7). God's liking us made God become like us.

That transformation of God, which we know as the Incarnation, convinces us that our God is a God who enjoys our joy; who mourns our sorrows; for whom we make a significant, sometimes tragic, difference. Still, can we promote and enhance the existence of this God? We can and do as we make the divine presence among us visible and tangible—even as Jesus did.

Can we talk of resembling God? Again, yes. That proposition is certainly less blasphemous sounding than the talk of God's resembling us. Resembling God is a by-product of the Incarnation. In the Word-made-flesh we see that human nature is capable of totally revealing the Godhead.[3] We know that we can be like God, because one of us *is* God. Moreover, the saints who have gone before us and those who still live among us offer evidence that we can become God-like in our sojourn here. We see these heroes begin to resemble the God of their commitment, yet not with the perfect freedom of being who they want to be. All of them would say, "I have missed the mark" (I am a sinner.) But their lives become touchstones of God's presence in our midst.

Before all else, to commit means to promise to "do" something. To be committed is to be commissioned (*promissio* involves *missio*).[4] It is to undertake a mission, which in its broadest outlines is the enhancement of that to which we are committed. I propose that it is among those who understand themselves in a reflective and selfless way as missionaries[5] that we will be best able to probe what being a committed and, therefore, commissioned Christian means today.

Scholars tell us that the concluding verses of Matthew's gospel constitute the mission of the earliest Christians as they conceived it.[6]

> All authority in heaven and on earth has been given to me. Go therefore and make disciples of all nations, baptizing them in the name of the Father and of the Son and of the Holy Spirit, and teaching them to obey everything that I have commanded you: and remember I am with you always to the end of the age.
>
> *Matthew 28:18–20*

It is still the mission of Christians committed to God, but its realization in today's world has undergone a number of changes.[7] As a base line for looking at these changes, consider as typical the mission described by a newly founded religious order in 1925: "The conversion of heathen in pagan lands."[8]

The simplicity, not to mention the language of such mission statements, have not survived a number of events and realizations. Perhaps the first of these is ecumenism. The World Council of Churches, the foremost ecumenical organization today, began with a meeting in Edinburgh in 1919 to address the scandalous undermining of mission by denominations competing for converts. The cooperation among the various Christian traditions issuing from that and subsequent meetings was institutionalized in 1948 in the World Council of Churches. For some, this had the effect of relativizing the different traditions among those cooperating. It did not seem to matter as it once had which Christian community one embraced.[9]

The emergence of former colonies of the major Western powers into sovereign nations, which began after World War II and continues into our own time, fostered another realization. Much mission work had been a form of colonializing. Theologians from the classically described missionary territories drag us to this embarrassing conclusion. Read Mercy Oduyoye of Ghana:

What comes through to the Africans who read the history of the missionary efforts of Europeans in Africa is the ethnocentricity of the account. It

142

was an exercise in cultural occupation. In fact missionary accounts often speak of "occupying" or "reoccupying" towns. The missionaries gave people names that only the Europeans could pronounce "correctly" because they found African names too difficult to say, or too heathen to enter into their Book of Life, which their God kept in their heaven.[10]

Finally, although much more heavily debated, there has been a recognition of the intrinsic value of religious traditions other than the Christian tradition. We find Peter foreshadowing that insight in Acts: "I truly understand that God shows no partiality, but in every nation anyone who fears him and does what is right is acceptable" (Acts 10:34–35). In context, this statement intends to reinforce the idea that no culture is inimical to the Word of God, rather than suggest that other religions are acceptable. But Christians had long questioned the anomaly of a good God denying salvation to those who had never heard of Christ or, if after being exposed to the Christian story, had not in conscience been able to embrace it.[11] There was always a school of teaching among Christians that if Peter was not talking about salvation outside the Church, he should have been.

A document issued by Vatican II in 1965 seemed to substantiate and canonize that conviction. The document, *The Relationship of the Church to Non-Christian Religions* (*Nostra aetate*), insisted that the Church "rejects nothing of what is true and holy in religions." It further counseled Her children:

143

to enter with prudence and charity into discussion and collaboration with members of other religions. Let Christians, while witnessing to their own faith and way of life, acknowledge, preserve and encourage the spiritual and moral truths found among non-Christians, also their social life and culture.[12]

In fact, that openness was modified in other documents issued by the Council. Meanwhile, the attempt to issue a similar statement by the World Council of Churches at Vancouver (1983) met vigorous resistance. The thesis of the document *Our Relation to People of Other Religious Convictions* as originally presented to the Assembly read:

While affirming the uniqueness of the birth, life, death and resurrection of Jesus to which we bear witness, we recognize God's creative work in the religious experience of people of other faiths.

The version finally published stated:

While affirming the uniqueness of the birth, life, death and resurrection of Jesus to which we bear witness, we recognize God's creative work in the *seeking for religious truth* among people of other faiths.[13]

Among missionaries themselves however, those from the mainline Churches at least, a consensus has been forming. Willie Jenkinson, an influential missiologist, captures this consensus: "It is no longer sufficient to say

144

that the missionary brings salvation or grace or God. These are already to be found where the missionary goes."[14] This realization may be even more dramatic than the recognition that dawned among the earliest Christians that they did not have to be Jews. Such insights seem to move us to a more awesome God, a God beyond our tribal gods. In any case, more and more missionaries describe their work as preparing for the reign of God, giving witness, and engaging in dialogue among themselves and with persons of other or no religious tradition. If, as I maintain, the commission of the missionary is our commission, it behooves us to study that vocation more closely.

Preparing for the Reign of God

Biblical scholarship[15] and prayerful reflection on the gospels have heightened our awareness of Jesus' own sense of mission, particularly as he identifies with the mission statement from Isaiah:

> The Spirit of the Lord is upon me, because he has anointed me to bring good news to the poor. He has sent me to proclaim release to the captives and recovery of sight to the blind, to let the oppressed go free, to proclaim the year of the Lord's favor.
>
> *Luke 4:18–19*

We are recapturing Jesus' emphasis on the coming reign of God—the kingdom. He proclaimed it: "The kingdom of God has come near" (Mark 1:15). "The kingdom of God is among you" (Luke 17:21). He described it in the parables and the beatitudes. He practiced it (as one practices law or medicine). And in the end, he died for it. His descriptions and prescriptions characterize the reign of God as authentic community and peace with justice. Like all the graced moments I have been describing, like understanding, conversion, commitment, or perserverance, we cannot of ourselves bring about the fullness of time when God will be all in all. But again we can do the equivalent of lighting sparklers, singing songs and the eschaton may come. There is therefore, a new, even central, emphasis among missionaries on "preparing for the Kingdom."[16]

In one sense, however, this is not a new work. Missionaries have always run schools, hospitals, and dispensaries. They have a long history of relieving suffering, of coming to the aid of victims. Novel to our times is an awareness of the systemic creation of victimhood. Ethnocentricism, political structures, and economic strategies oppress whole peoples. Freeing people from these burdens is now seen as integral to preparing for the kingdom.

But the tradition of relieving victims and eliminating victimhood is not uniquely Christian, even if our vocabulary and motivation is.[17] A glance at the work of the United Nations, secular organizations such as the Red Cross and Red Crescent, or Amnesty International, even the efforts of entertainers in Comic Relief or Live Aid suggests that being one another's keepers and stewards of the galaxy is the human vocation. Which is not surprising if to be human is to be God-like.

Insight into the causes of victimhood has made some missionaries political activists. Those in conservative denominations are more likely to see such activism as a distraction from what they still conceive to be their main task: making converts. But missionaries in the mainline churches rarely define their mission that way. Their interaction with persons from other religions is currently described under the rubrics of witness and dialogue.

They prepare for the reign of God by witnessing to its values, by living in solidarity with the poor and oppressed and abandoned. The mission statement of one group describes this witness: "In the diversity of their cultures we walk with them along roads down which their own lives call them. We adopt lifestyles in harmony with theirs."[18] This form of mission can be traced back at least as far as St. Francis of Assisi's rule for his friars among the Saracens. But dialogue as a form of mission is novel.

Dialogue

In its *Guidelines for Dialogue,* the members of the World Council of Churches assure their partners in dialogue that they come "not as manipulators but as fellow pilgrims."[19] Questions, not answers, are to be the subject of the conversations. Some evangelical denominations have another view of dialogue however: "In true dialogue, we seek both to disclose the inadequacies and falsities of non-Christian religions and to demonstrate the adequacy and truth, the absoluteness and finality of the Lord Jesus Christ."[20]

In these two views of dialogue, we find the nub of current disagreements among missioners. It hinges on the truth-claims of Christianity especially those that claim a radical uniqueness in Christianity and the finality of Christ. Leslie Newbigin, a revered missionary, puts one side of the debate succinctly:

> "How and where is God's purpose for the whole of creation and the human family made visible and credible?" That is the question about the truth—objective truth—which is true whether or not it coincides with my "values." And I know of no other place in the public history of the world where the dark mystery of human life is illuminated, and the dark power of all that denies human well-being is met and measured and mastered, except in those events that have their focus in what happened "under Pontius Pilate."[21]

The title of a collection of essays reflects the position of those who hold a diametrically opposed view: *The Myth of a Christian Uniqueness: Toward a Pluralistic Theology of Religions*. The authors explore the ramifications of "a move away from insistence on the superiority or finality of Christ and Christianity toward a recognition of the independent validity of other ways."[22]

Several different explanations have been offered to explain the explicit claims of uniqueness and finality found in the scriptures and tradition. One is the paradoxical universality of that claim.[23] The sense of chosenness, of uniqueness, can be found among all peoples. The word *Bantu* for example means human. Anyone not Bantu was not human. The earliest Europeans in North America considered themselves to be chosen people in a promised land. As the world shrinks, as chosen people keep meeting other chosen people, the claim becomes hollow.

Another explanation holds that the Graeco-Roman empire's view of itself as universal and containing the one true humanistic culture may have contributed directly to that claim in scripture and tradition.[24] Yet another explanation of the exclusivist language of scripture is that it is the rhetoric of love. "It is the sort of language a husband uses when he tells his wife that she is the most beautiful woman in the world or when a wife tells her husband that he is the only one for her."[25]

Whether one embraces Newbigin's position (Christianity is the one true religion) or that of the authors of *The Myth of Christian Uniqueness* (there are many true religions, or another version, there is one religion that takes many "true" forms), one must simultaneously embrace a notion of truth that I maintain is no longer tenable. Another approach, however, restores the centrality of evangelizing (proclaiming the faith as opposed to propagating it)[26] without deemphasizing preparation for the kingdom, witness, or dialogue. I believe that studying the missionary commission (*our* commission) to evangelize from the perspective of beauty can inform the quality and depth of our commitment.

Evangelizing from the Perspective of Beauty

Evangel literally means "good news" as, of course, does *gospel*, its English translation. This very designation lends itself more to beauty than to truth. The refrain that accompanies the first creation story, "And God saw that it was good," and concludes the account, "God saw everything that he had made, and indeed, it was very good" (Genesis 1:31) refers to a "good" that is aesthetic, not moral. There are not good or evil skies or moons or fish. It must be the good that means beauty. Then, "Behold it was very good" could be translated "And God said, 'Ahh!'" Although the Good News of the gospel has obvious moral and therefore political dimensions, an aesthetic approach does not compromise these dimensions as I tried to demonstrate in Chapter Two.

Yet, a number of reservations surface at the prospect of considering religious traditions from the perspective of beauty rather than truth. First, there is the obvious argument: it is really *good* news only if it is true. But the awesome, even awful, claims of the Christian tradition are acquiring credibility. They are proving their trustworthiness through time. Only at the eschaton will we know that in fact they correspond to reality. As James says, "There are no conclusions. For what has concluded that we may conclude about it?" Moreover, the truth in either the correspondence or the dependable theories is not intrinsically desirable. It may always be useful, but we can sympathize with someone who says, "I do not want to know the truth; it is too painful." Since beauty is always life-enhancing, it would be harder to conceive of someone saying, "I don't want to see the beautiful." Truth is instrumental; beauty is consummatory. We use truth, but we rest in beauty. Beauty is a form of the good; it is the good perceived. To put it in a Thomistic context: Beauty is to knowing what the good is to desire.[27]

That beauty does not, at first glance, have the energizing power of truth and falsity might be another reservation. I am inclined to say that is not so bad. The atrocities committed in the name of religious or political truth make me think that we are well rid of that energy. On the other hand, the discipline, even deprivation, to which artists submit in their pursuit of beauty is axiomatic. Perhaps more to the strain of our discussion is the record that a whiff of beauty has launched innumerable scientists on the scent of a theory or project that consumed years of their energy—often in the face of disconfirming evidence. Dirac wrote, "It is more important to have beauty in one's equations than to have them fit the experiment."[28] Not that scientists are disinterested in the "fit." Rather, as one commentator concluded:

> These scientists express essentially the faith that what the mind perceives as beautiful finds its realization in nature, that is, the beauty of a scientific theory implies its truth. [And in fact] Theories which they created on what were considered primarily aesthetic grounds were later confirmed experimentally.[29]

In other words, the beauty of a vision can commit us to its verification process.

That beauty is purely subjective is a classic reservation. "In the eye of the beholder" we say, the implication being *only* in that beholder's eye. Beauty like that other great place holder in our language—love—seems to frustrate our attempts to define it in a way that secures general agreement. As a result, the concept of beauty has been neglected in our century where we would expect to see it—in aesthetic theory. In the major indexes, most of the citations under the subject of beauty have to do with cosmetology! I am very indebted, therefore, in this section to the work of Mary Mothersill, a philosophy professor at Barnard College, particularly as found in her aptly named *Beauty Restored*.[30] I would like to back into a more extended discussion of beauty, however, by first exploring an analogy for religious traditions.

AN ANALOGY FOR RELIGIOUS TRADITIONS

Let us think of a religious tradition as the score of a masterpiece *as well as* the musicians who perform the music, interpreting and playing the score. What they make possible is our experience of the music. It is the music that is beautiful, the music we love. We may cherish the composer, appreciate the musicianship of the performers, acknowledge that both the score and performance are the conditions of experiencing the music, but it is still the music whose beauty arrests us.

As with all analogies, there are limits to how far this one can take us.[31] A musical masterpiece is, after all, *not* a religious tradition. Yet, similarities present themselves. For example, all religious traditions exist to put us in touch with God. It is the reality of God in which we are called to revel, not the tradition. The "Good News" therefore is the God whom we touch or, better, who touches us in the Christian tradition. The tradition is constituted by the score (scriptures, creeds, and rituals) performed by different peoples with different interpretations for over two thousand years.

I will not explore every aspect of the analogy, as fruitful as that might be. In the hope of providing a fresh and effective perspective on our own commitment as Christians, I will confine myself to those aspects that address some current issues of mission.

First, what should the musician (the missionary) do? Perform the score of course. The notations of a musical score may not kill, but they are certainly lifeless. They exist to be performed.

The analogy speaks to the issue of relativism discussed in Chapter Two. Not every interpretation of the score or every performance is uniformly admirable. Interpretations that wander too far from the original score court criticism from the musically informed; the grossly ill-performed is often recognized even by nonmusicians. Yet, novel arrangements or the use of new or different instruments can make it into the canon of good performances over time. The point is that there are standards of interpretation and criteria for performance that proscribe "anything goes." But they do not rule out the novel or an agreement upon new standards and criteria that the novel frequently generates.

The analogy of religious traditions with performed masterpieces illuminates the issue of dialogue in mission. What musician worthy of the name is not open to hearing the beauty of other masterpieces or other interpretations of familiar works? In theory at least, musicians are open to critiques of their performances as well as critiques of their judgment about a masterpiece.

Yet their very familiarity with and practiced performance of a beloved masterpiece is what can engage another to see the beauty they see, to hear the beauty they hear—perhaps to recognize it as a masterpiece. The other may recognize that fact though never contract to perform the piece.

The analogy of the performed masterpiece also sheds some light on denominational affiliation and the issue of transcending cultures. One can treasure a particular masterpiece and a particular interpretation and performance of that masterpiece for all kinds of personal reasons that are no less providential for being personal. We are born into a particular time and place with its culture and its variations on our block and in our house. That fact both discovers and conceals the world to us. It conditions what foods we will enjoy, how we will be educated, whom we will marry, even if we will marry. The conventions of a culture shape what we will find agreeable and disagreeable; what we will pursue and what we will not notice or, having noticed, dismiss out of hand.

So musicians are more likely to treasure a masterpiece from their own culture. They are predisposed, as it were, to discern beauty there. As they grow in their knowledge of music and increase their skill in performing a masterpiece, they will continue to get fresh insights into its unique beauty if it can bear that sustained familiarity. If it cannot, they may look to another masterpiece for experience of the sublime.

There is no doubt that we are culturally conditioned to resonate to certain chords, certain kinds of melodies. But perhaps we make too much of that conditioning. If our cultures distinguish us, even separate us, our common humanity defines and connects us. If we eat different foods, we all have to eat, and we all need the same nutrients to sustain us, no matter their form. If we all have different languages, we all have languages. If we all have different wedding customs, we all marry. And we all make music. And we all have gods—or at least ultimate concerns.

Cultural oppression exists where we try to make people take their nutrients in our form, speak our language, use our marriage customs, dance to our rhythms. We, in the North Atlantic community moving towards the third millennium of the Common Era, sometimes forget that the notes that constitute the motif of our masterpiece come from an old Middle Eastern tribal melody. Its adaptability into thousands of languages and cultures stems from the fact that it strikes notes common to the human condition: birth, death, life after death, love and God. Is beauty another common note?

Let us consider beauty as *an aesthetic quality whose apprehension in itself causes pleasure and inspires love.*[32] I will examine each of these elements in turn, beginning with aesthetic quality. John Dewey has mapped the nature of quality in a helpful way. For him the notion of quality is identical with aesthetic quality:

> Quality is the affectional and emotional hue that pervades an experience making it *this* experience. In what is termed a situation, an immediate quality pervades everything that enters into that situation. If the situation is that of being lost in a forest, the quality of being lost permeates and affects every detail that is observed and thought of. The "parts" are such only qualitatively.[33]

We are more used to the term referring to the arts. We speak of a musical piece as being Brahmsian or of the Titian quality of a painting. Dewey again: "The word thus used certainly does not refer to any particular line, color or part of the painting. It is something that affects and modifies all the constituents of the picture and all of their relations. It is not anything that can be expressed in words for it is something that must be *had*."[34]

Mothersill describes apprehension as a "cognitive success,"[35] an accurate grasp of an object—as opposed to a misapprehension. "Sufficient acquaintance"[36] is another description for apprehension. But "in itself" is the essential note. Apprehension of something as beautiful may include many elements that cause pleasure and inspire love—the poem was dedicated to me, my best friend is conducting the symphony. But, when apprehension *itself* pleases, *anyone* apprehending the object can expect to be delighted. It *is* beautiful.

The pleasure derived from the apprehension of beauty is marked by intensity, duration, and fecundity. The intensity of delight or force of pleasure endures extended and extensive apprehension of the object (person, poem, or God). Moreover such apprehension fosters creative activity. "We know a man for a poet," says Mothersill quoting Coleridge, "from the fact he makes us poets."[37]

Finally, and wonderfully, beauty inspires love of what is apprehended as distinct from the pleasure of apprehending. In other words, this intense, enduring, and fecund pleasure is the signal that we are in the presence of beauty, but we love that which is beautiful, not the signal of its presence.

This last aspect gives us another point of entry into the discussion. When we speak of a beautiful person, as distinct from a beautiful-looking person, we are referring to some quality that pervades her or his being. Were we asked why we make this claim, we might describe a variety of actions that indicate care; words that are consoling, wise, challenging; attitudes of healthy self-deprecation. Yet not one of these descriptions or their aggregate captures the quality because beauty is the way the person is; it is an adverb that modifies the person's be-ing in the world.

We simultaneously imply in our claim that continued acquaintance with this person will only foster the conviction of beauty. We also imply that existence is enhanced by knowing this person. We are saying in effect: "This person is lovable." To know (apprehend) this person is to love him or her—apart from anything gratifying that the person does for us. (A peculiar feature of the Good News God is that this God finds us intrinsically beautiful. We are loved unconditionally, loved apart from anything we do or say.)

There may not be a word for beauty in every language, but certainly there are experiences, the qualities of which please in themselves apart from every other consideration, a pleasure that endures extended apprehension and fosters creative activity. Unfortunately, there are those whose intense pain, whether of hunger, oppression, or personal tragedy, drastically constrict their capacity for this kind of pleasure. They give us our priority in mission. If, as the World Council insists, "Everyone is entitled to hear the Good News,"[38] they are *first* entitled to the capacity to hear it. Moreover, everything in the score dictates that priority.[39]

The point of the discussion so far has been to make a case for evangelizing, not only as dialogue, but as *proclaiming* the Good News, the God revealed in the Christian Tradition. For that, the definition of beauty may not seem helpful. Quality by definition is ineffable; God by definition is ungraspable.

Although quality cannot be expressed in words, it can be alluded to in ways that help others to experience it similarly. Good art critics are those who have mastered that power of allusion. They say things like, "Look at the grace of that line." "See how that color expresses the peace of the scene." They hope by their words, by their directions for perceiving, to enable us to see the beauty they see. Mothersill says that "critical exposition is an art akin to pedagogy and, like pedagogy, takes training, practice, concentration and skill."[40]

So does evangelism.

Another way of evoking the recognition of quality that evangelists might consider is the flip side of consciousness raising. In consciousness raising, by means of conversation, exposure to programmed experiences, and the study of history, people are made aware of the pervasive quality of oppression in their lives due to racism, sexism, or classism—sometimes all three. Similar methods might be used to make people aware of the beauty of God in their lives.[41]

From another perspective, the God of the Good News is uniquely graspable. This God is God-with-us. The Incarnation reveals that our planetary "stuff" is drenched with Deity. The Eucharist is not an exception to the rest of reality, but a clue to it. The score tells us that we grasp God when we grasp anyone. This very graspability reinforces the priority of mission as the overcoming of injustice. The passion and death of Jesus convinces us that anyone's passion is God's pain, that God's Beloved is crucified by any injustice. But justice is not simply the absence of injustice. We are commissioned not only to eliminate injustice but to establish justice. Matthew Fox artfully defines justice as "the structured struggle to share the pleasure of God's good earth."[42] Evangelism is the structured struggle to share the pleasure of the good earth's God. Evangelizing still makes wonderful sense in an age of pluralism.

So far, I have described the meaning of commitment and looked at the missionary vocation of those committed to the Good News God. The issue now is how does one keep on keeping on? Can we nurture the intense conversion explored in Chapters Three and Four, such that we are transformed?

NURTURING COMMITMENT

Affect is a funny thing. "The honeymoon will end," we warn newly wedded couples and newly converted friends. Passion waxes and wanes. We can come to experience even our commitment to God as grim duty. We can lose the joy of exercising our commission. Members of Roman Catholic religious orders who vow their commitment to God in a public ritual regularly recite a "Prayer for the Grace of Final Perseverance." That recitation recognizes that pledging oneself simply places us on the course we intend to follow. If we persevere to the end, it will be, as so much else that is significant in life, gift, grace. But the recitation also recognizes that that does not mean there is nothing we can do. We can at least pray. And there are other means of nurturing perseverance in our commitment.

Some years ago Rosabeth Moss Kanter examined nineteenth century utopian communities to distill from the records what she described as the mechanisms of commitment.[43] She listed them as sacrifice (one gives up something valuable), investment (time, energy and/or money is put into the commitment), renunciation (association with persons outside the community is proscribed or circumscribed), communion (a sense of oneness with the group is promoted), mortification (strategies of social control wear away at the individual's identity), and transcendence (surrender to the authority of the group is fostered by cultivating an awe for the institution).

As described by Kanter and as practiced in contemporary cults, these mechanisms seem repellently manipulative to us today. Yet, the "Twelve Step Programs," so popular worldwide and so helpful to those committed to a sober self, incorporate versions of all these mechanisms. Perhaps the difference is that the strategies as Kanter describes them are used to promote commitment to an organization rather than to a principle or a person. Perhaps that kind of commitment is the defining note of cults. In any case, the successful use of these mechanisms by "anonymous" groups suggests that they can be adapted so that they do strengthen our intentions.

On the other hand, the asceticism of commitment outlined by Margaret A. Farley is unambiguously helpful.

I must acknowledge her influence throughout this chapter. She in turn acknowledges her debt to the philosopher Gabriel Marcel. She finds Marcel's distinction between constancy and fidelity especially illuminating.

Marcel uses the term *constancy* to describe the commitment we experience as grim duty and contrasts constancy with fidelity, which he describes as imbued with "presence."[44] He goes on to say that we are likely to be constant for ourselves. "I said I would be here, and here I am. I could not live with myself if I did not show up." But fidelity involves being present for the other "and more precisely for thou."[45] Farley is concerned with ways to cultivate this "presence" in our commitments. I adapt and extend her suggestions under the headings of re-membering, relaxing, and relating.

Re-membering

Re-membering involves recalling and putting together. Our most common use of *remember* means recalling something—an event, a person, a telephone number. But what kind of memory nourishes presence in commitment? Farley calls it the original vision.[46] Because we no longer see what first compelled our commitment, does not mean it is no longer there. Because we no longer experience the heady moments (or years) of "release, emergence, breakthrough, acceptance, birth"[47] that marked our conversion does not mean that their Cause is no longer there.

It has been stated often enough to have the quality of a truism that we are usually right in affirming what we see and frequently wrong in claiming nonexistence for what we do not see. We may have closed our eyes from exhaustion, grown weary of wonders as Chesterton said, or tired of beholding beauty. Sometimes, as Charles Williams wrote "Beauty ceases in one's own sight to be beauty and the revelation to be revelation."[48]

Undoubtedly, what we initially experienced was there. Recalling that original vision may energize our capacity to experience it again, freshly, enlarged. Amazing Grace. "How precious did that grace appear, the hour I first believed."

Re-membering can also mean putting the parts together. A creative fidelity involves the asceticism of putting our lives together in such a way that space and time are cleared for cultivating and celebrating our original vision of the Good News God and, just as importantly, for making new memories.

Relaxing

Relaxing involves putting play into our commitment and our belief. Commitment is work. When we talk about working at our commitment to God, we would like to think that it is work in the sense of an *oeuvre*, but too often it may simply be work in the sense of drudgery. Yet we know that straining at our work not only causes all kinds of aches in our body, it can also undermine the work. Farley calls relaxation the center of patience, the patience we need to pace our selves in a lifetime commitment.[49]

I suggest that there is a relaxation that comes from putting play into our commitment—*play* meaning the give we refer to when we speak of the play in a steering wheel. The tightening of our muscles, the hardening of our hearts, the squinting of our eyes can prevent our being present and creative in our fidelity. The stiffening of our body-soul makes us impatient with the celebration of the original vision or the making of new memories.

Perhaps nothing relaxes us more than laughter. Creative fidelity is well served by wit, a word based on the same root from which we get vision and wisdom. It is significant that Arthur Koestler, in his classic work on creativity, begins with a study of humor. Koestler describes the source of humor (and creativity) as bisociative thinking, "perceiving a situation or event in two habitually incompatible associative contexts."[50] Christianity seems intrinsically humorous: One God who is three, a God who becomes human, a virgin mother, a human Mother of God.

Which brings me to another area of commitment requiring play. The beliefs that ground or mediate our commitment must, I think, have play in them—a certain looseness so that God can be God. How many commitments have been subverted by constricted beliefs, personal commitments that turned out to be only a commitment to a cross section of the other person's history? The subject of the commitment was not allowed to grow or surprise us. Lack of play in our beliefs can even forestall commitment. For example, in John's gospel, we find some people of Jerusalem on the verge of commitment. "Can it be that the authorities really know that this is the Messiah? Yet we know where this man is from; but when the Messiah comes, no one will know where he is from" (John 7:26–27).

Relating

Relating involves the cultivation of community, *ecclesia*. Sociologists of knowledge have made us aware that we cannot believe anything by ourselves. We need plausibility structures, "social confirmation for our beliefs about reality."[51] The need for a community to help us sustain commitment to our beliefs has been well documented. What I would like to focus on here then is the need for community to (1) spell us in commitment and (2) foster *disbelief* when it is appropriate.

1. We need a community to sustain a creative fidelity when as individuals, we seem capable only of constancy. The Rule of St. Basil talks about needing a group to do all that we are commanded to do because "For example when we visit a sick person we cannot [at the same time] receive a stranger." When we minister at a distance we must neglect our work at home, and so on.[52] The *ecclesia* enables us to do what we want to do and should do, but cannot because of our finitude. In our local communities, brothers and sisters can carry our commitment. When our juices are spent, when we have grown "weary of wonders" and "tired of beholding beauty," others can keep the vigil for us while we sleep. And then they can awaken us. They can inspire us literally by breathing new life into our commitment by example.

   We see this occurring on a worldwide basis. The believers in the developing nations are revivifying the commitment of the believers in the unraveling nations. The original vision is still fresh in their memory and they refresh our faith grown stale, if not cynical. I think that we in the West and especially in the North are absolutely dependent upon them to awaken us and inspire us.

2. But we also need *ecclesia* to foster disbelief when it is appropriate, to chasten our commitment. We know that we need a community to believe. We are not usually as conscious of our need for community in order to disbelieve. In fact, we are more likely to believe too much than too little. Our beliefs are inclined to be too cluttered, too detailed. We include belief about the Messiah's birthplace in our belief in the Messiah. Basil again reminds us that by ourselves we do not readily recognize our defects. We need others to reprove us with kindness and compassion. We need a community who will respond as Jesus did to the overbelief of those people in Jerusalem. "You know me, and you know where I come from?" (John 7:28). You must be joking.

Liturgy is the preeminent nourishment of conversion and commitment. The assembly for worship, particularly in the Eucharist, is characterized by re-membering, relaxing, and relating. We make space and time to remember the original vision and make new memories. We cultivate a community that can spell us when we fall asleep in the vigil, and we hear our beliefs critiqued against the Christian story/Christian score. Finally, the liturgy promotes relaxation by celebrating our conviction that no matter how tragic our personal circumstances, how prevalent evil seems in the world—we are players in a comedy. (The very word *comedy* implies a messianic image, coming as it does from the Greek meaning originally a banquet with singing!) Evil and death will not have the last word. Existence has a happy ending.

E P I L O G U E

❉

John put down the book. He prayed for a long, long, long time. Then he left the house.

ENDNOTES

PROLOGUE

1. See Robert W. Funk, Roy W. Hoover, and the Jesus Seminar, *The Search for the Authentic Words of Jesus* (New York: Polebridge Press (Macmillan), 1993.
2. Corita Kent in Harvey Cox, *The Feast of Fools: A Theological Essay on Festivity and Fantasy* (Cambridge: Harvard University Press, 1969), 108.

INTRODUCTION

1. Craig Blomberg in *The Globalization of Theological Education.* Robert A. Evans, Alice F. Evans and David A. Roozen, eds. (Maryknoll, NY: Orbis, 1993), 222–223.
2. Eugene A. Nida, *Toward a Science of Translating* (Leiden: E.J. Brill, 1964), 166. See also E.A. Nida and C.R. Tabor, *The Theory and Practice of Translation* (Leiden: E.J. Brill, 1969), 24.
3. Private conversation with Professor Joseph Osei-Bonsu of Accra University, Ghana (now, Bishop of Konongo-Mampong).
4. Leonardo Boff, *New Evangelization: Good News to the Poor* (Maryknoll, NY: Orbis, 1991), 8.

5. Josiah U. Young, *Black and African Theologies: Siblings or Distant Cousins* (Maryknoll, NY: Orbis, 1986). Young sees African theology emphasizing indigenization (Mbiti, Fashole-Luke, Harry Sawyerr, F. Eboussi Boulanga), whereas Black theologies emphasize liberation (Kelly Brown, James Cone, Major Jones J. Deotis Roberts, Cecil Cone).

6. James T. Borhek and Richard F. Curtis, *A Sociology of Belief* (Malabar, FL: Robert E. Krieger, 1983), 51–52.

7. John Coulson, *Religion and Imagination* (Oxford: Clarendon Press, 1981), 4.

8. I. Howard Marshal, "Culture and the New Testament," *Gospel and Culture*. John Stott and Robert. T. Coote, eds. (Pasadena, CA: William Carey Library, 1979), 29.

9. Robert J. Schreiter, "A Framework for a Discussion of Inculturation," *Mission in Dialogue* Mary Motte, F.M.M. and Joseph Lang, M.M., eds. (Maryknoll, NY: Orbis, 1982), 546.

CHAPTER 1

1. William James, *Pragmatism and Other Essays*, (New York: Washington Square Press, 1963), 5. James quotes Chesterton to make the point I am making here.

2. Charles Glock, "Consciousness Among Contemporary Youth: An Interpretation," in *The New Religious Consciousness*, ed. Charles Y. Block and Robert N. Bellah (Berkeley: University of California Press, 1976), 353.

3. Alfred North Whitehead, *Process and Reality: An Essay in Cosmology* (New York: Macmillan, 1936), Part II, 1, 1.

4. Mircea Eliade, *Cosmos and History: The Myth of the Eternal Return*, trans. Willard R. Trask (New York: Harper & Brothers, Harper Torchbooks), 1959), 34.

5. Augustine, *Contra Julian*, IV 14, 72; P1 44, 774.

6. James Ross, "Unless You Believe You Will Not Understand," in Eugene Thomas Long, ed. *Experience, Reason and God* (Washington, D.C.: The Catholic University of America Press, 1980), 118.

7. John J. McDermott, "The American Angle of Vision" *Cross Currents* (Winter, 1965), 69.

8. Edmundo O'Gorman, *The Invention of America: An Inquiry into the Historical Nature of the New World and the Meaning of its History*, (Bloomington, IN: Indiana University Press, 1961), 58– 69.

9. Augustine, *City of God*, XVI 7,8,9, 17.

10. O'Gorman, *The Invention of America*, 137

11. Ibid., 170.

12. Ibid., 122.

13. Ibid., 168–169.

14. Jacob Bronowski, *Ascent of Man* (Boston: Little Brown and Co., 1973), 197.

15. Stillman Drake, *Galileo at Work: His Scientific Biography* (Chicago: The University of Chicago Press, 1978), 345. Italics mine.

16. Stillman Drake, *Galileo* (New York: Hill and Wang, 1980), 5.

17. Drake, *Galileo at Work*, 356. Although the expression is usually considered a legend attached to the story of Galileo's trial, Drake is convinced that Galileo did in fact say this, but not at the time of the trial. In Belgium in 1911, a 1643 painting of Galileo in prison was discovered to have the famous sentence on a part of the canvas that had been folded behind the picture. Drake considers the expression quite in character, although the story could not begin to be told until after Galileo's death for fear of the Inquisition.

18. I Bernard Cohen, *Revolution in Science* (Cambridge, MA: Harvard University Belknap Press, 1985), 148.

19. Recounted in Ian Barbour, *Issues in Science and Religion* (New York: Prentice Hall, 1966; New York: Harper and Row, Harper Torchbooks, 1971), 58.

20. The American Declaration of Independence is a textbook example of experience as the ground of knowledge. "Truths" are "self-evident." That is, available to anyone's experience.

21. Nick Roddick, "Oh What a Lovely War" *McGill's Survey of Cinema*, Second Series, Vol. 4, Frank N. McGill, ed. (Englewood, NJ: Sallem Press, 1981).

22. William Butler Yeats, "The Second Coming," *The Collected Poems of W.B. Yeats* (New York: Macmillan, 1956), 184.

23. I Bernard Cohen, *Revolution*, 411.

24. Cited in Norma Thompson, "Art and the Religious Experience," *Aesthetic Dimensions of Religious Education*. Gloria Durka and Joanmarie Smith, eds. (New York: Paulist Press, 1979), 44.

25. Max Born, "Physics and Metaphysics" *Scientific Monthly* 82, 5 (May, 1956), 234. Italics mine.

26. Ellen K. Coughlin, "Kuhn's Revolutionary Book," *Chronicle of Higher Education*, 1982. Such a revolutionary re-view of the scientific method had been suggested by other philosophers (e. g. Michael Polanyi) and historians (e.g. Herbert Butterfield). But none made the profound and broad impression that Kuhn did.

27. Thomas S. Kuhn, *The Structure of Scientific Revolutions* Second Edition, Enlarged (Chicago: The University of Chicago Press, 1970), 1.

28. Norwood Hanson, *Patterns of Discovery* (Cambridge: Cambridge University Press, 1958), 18.

29. Kuhn, *Structure*, 158.

30. Ibid., 118–119

31. Richard J. Bernstein, *Beyond Objectivism and Relativism: Science, Hermeneutics, and Praxis* (Philadelphia, PA: University of Pennsylvania Press, 1983), 51.

32. Margaret Masterman, "The Nature of a Paradigm," *Criticism and Growth of Knowledge*, Imre Lakatos and Alan Musgrave, eds. (New York: Cambridge University Press, 1970), 61–65. As a result of this criticism, Kuhn seems to have backed away from the notion of paradigm in his subsequent work. He has tried to substitute "disciplinary matrix," but unsucessfully. See "Reflections on My Critics," in *Criticism and Growth of Knowledge*, 271. See also Thomas S. Kuhn, *The Essential Tension: Selected Studies in Scientific Tradition and Change* (Chicago: The University of Chicago Press, 1977), 393–394.

33. I Bernard Cohen, *Revolution*, 578.

CHAPTER 2

1. Ray L. Hart, *Unfinished Man and the Imagination: Toward an Ontology and a Rhetoric of Revelation* (New York: Herder and Herder, 1968), 186–187.

2. William James, *Psychology: Briefer Course* (New York: Henry Holt & Co., 1892), 29.

3. The theory of knowing that is outlined in this chapter is sometimes called "critical realism." Two scholars in religious studies who explicitly use this theory are Ian Barbour and John Hick. See for example: "The critical realist recognizes the importance of human imagination in the formation of theories and acknowledges the incomplete and selective character of scientific theories. . . . Descriptions of nature are human constructions but nature is such as to bear description in some ways and not others." Ian G. Barbour, *Myths, Models and Paradigms: A Comparative Study of Science and Religion* (New York: Harper and Row, 1974), 37.

The theory is also called a kind of neo-Kantianism. John Hick distinguishes it from Kantianism this way: "We necessarily perceive

172

the world as it appears to beings with our own particular kind of perceptual machinery. But the way in which it appears to human perceivers is the way it is in relation to human perceivers. In Kantian language, the phenomenal world is the noumenal world, as humanly experienced." John Hick, *Problems of Religious Pluralism* (New York: St. Martin's Press, 1985), 104–105. See also John Hick, *Faith and Knowledge* second edition (Ithaca, NY: Cornell University Press, 1966), 200–211.

4. Peter L. Berger and Thomas Luckmann, *The Social Construction of Reality: A Treatise in The Sociology of Knowledge* (Garden City, NY: Doubleday, 1966), 85ff.

5. In Thomas S. Kuhn, *The Structure of Scientific Revolutions* Second Edition, Enlarged (Chicago: University of Chicago Press, 1970), 151.

6. Two programs of research that have made great strides in this area are the studies at the University of Minnesota and the Center for Multiple Birth in Chicago. See Peter Watson, *Twins* (New York: Viking, 1981. See also Susan L. Farber, *Identical Twins Raised Apart: A Reanalysis* (New York: Basic Books, 1981.

7. Robert Ornstein, *The Psychology of Consciousness* (New York: Harcourt, Brace and Jovanovich, 1977), 8.

8. There is a pecking order in every discipline. Among scientists it has been called "physics envy."

9. Neils Bohr in K. C. Cole "A Theory of Everything," *The New York Times Magazine* (October 18, 1987), 22.

10. Stillman Drake, *Galileo at Work* (Chicago: The University of Chicago Press, 1978), 417.

11. E. N. da C. Andrade, *An Approach to Modern Physics* (Garden City, NY: Doubleday Anchor Books, 1957), 245.

12. Suzanne Langer, *Problems of Art* (New York: Charles Scribner's Sons, 1957), 80.

13. John Dewey, *Art as Experience* (New York: Capricorn Books, 1958 [1934], 3.

14. Ibid.

15. Hannah Arendt, *The Life of the Mind* One Volume Edition (New York: Harcourt, Brace Jovanovich, 1978), 3–6. Arendt describes how she was motivated to write this book by her attendance at the Eichmann trial in Jerusalem. At a loss to explain the motivation for his evil actions during the Nazi era, she finally concluded that his "thoughtlessness" was the source.

16. John Dewey, *Art as Experience*.

17. William Cantwell Smith, *Towards a World Theology: Faith and the Comparative History of Religion* (Philadelphia: The Westminster Press, 1981), 82.

18. Jaroslav Pelikan, *Jesus Through the Centuries: His Place in the History of Culture* (New York: Harper and Row, 1987 [1985]). See also his series *The Christian Tradition: A History of the Development of Doctrine* (Chicago: University of Chicago Press, 1971–1984).

19. John Hick has an essay where he makes many of these same points. See "On Grading Religions" in *Problems...*, 67–87.

20. Rosemary Radford Ruether speaks against the need to defend one's religion and instead, the responsibility to question it. "Asking the Existential Questions," *Theologians in Transition*, James M. Wall, ed. (New York: Crossroads, 1981), 165.

CHAPTER 3

1. Gilbert K. Chesterton cited in John Murray Cuddihy, *No Offense* (New York: Seabury Press, 1978), 37.

2. Robert N. Bellah, "Civil Religion in America," in *American Civil Religion*, eds. Russel E. Richey and Donald G. Jones (New York: Harper and Row, 1974), 22.

3. John E. Smith, "The Concept of Conversion," in *Conversion: Perspectives on Personal and Social Transformation*, ed. Walter E. Conn (New York: Alba House, 1978), 51–52.

4. David K. O'Rourke, O.P., "The Experience of Conversion," in *The Human Experience of Conversion: Persons and Structures in Transformation*, ed. Francis A. Eigo, O.S.A.(Villanova, PA: Villanova University Press, 1987), 13.

5. James W. Fowler, *Stages of Faith* (San Francisco: Harper and Row, 1981), 24–25.

6. Stuart D. McLean, "Basic Sources and New Possibilities: H Richard Niebuhr's Influence on Faith Development Theory," in *Faith Development and Fowler*, eds. Craig Dykstra and Sharon Parks (Birmingham, AL: Religious Education Press, 1986), 166.

7. Fowler, *Stages*, 281.

8. Walter E. Conn, *Christian Conversion: A Developmental Interpretation of Autonomy and Surrender* (New York: Paulist Press, 1986), 31.

9. Ibid., 208–209.

10. Mario Puzo, *The Godfather* (New York: Putnam, 1969).

11. "Faith and Order Trends," *NCCCUSA* 6 (September, 1966), 3.

12. William James, *The Varieties of Religious Experience* (Cambridge: Harvard University Press, 1985), 163.
13. Ibid., 162.
14. Ibid.
15. Molly Rush, "Living, Mothering, Resisting," in *Christianity and Crisis* (December 8, 1980), 348. See also Lianme Ellison Norman, "Living Up to Molly," ibid., 341–344.
16. Tad Trost, "Conversion: An Interview with Lew Rambo," *Chimes* 33 (Spring, 1988), 8–9. Rambo describes four kinds of conversion. 1) Tradition transition, the conversion from the Christian tradition to the Hindu tradition. 2) Institutional transition, conversion within a tradition. A Baptist becomes a Presbyterian. 3) Affiliation: someone with little or no commitment becomes involved with a faith community. 4) Intensification: "A person does not move institutionally...but, there is a new intensity or passion."
17. James F. Loder, *The Transforming Moment: Understanding Convictional Experiences* (San Francisco: Harper and Row, 1981), 31.
18. Ibid., 32.
19. Ibid., 33.
20. Maria Harris, *Teaching and Religious Imagination: An Essay in the Theology of Teaching* (San Francisco: Harper and Row, 1987), 25.
21. Ibid., 26.
22. Ibid., 30.
23. Ibid., 34.
24. Rosemary Haughton, *The Passionate God* (New York: Paulist Press, 1981), 35–36.
25. Rosemary Haughton, *The Transformation of Man* (New York: Paulist Press, 1967), 74.
26. Elisabeth Kubler Ross, *On Death and Dying* (New York: The Macmillan Co., 1969).
27. Jacques Pasquier, "Experience and Conversion," in *Conversion*, ed. Walter E. Conn. 198.
28. Stephanie Demetrakopoulos, *Listening to Our Bodies: The Rebirth of Feminine Wisdom* (Boston: Beacon Press, 1982), 20. See also Stanislav Grof, *Beyond the Brain: Birth, Death and Transcendence in Psychotherapy* (Albany: State University of New York, 1985), 102–127.
29. Sallie McFague, *Models of God: Theology for an Ecological, Nuclear Age* (Philadelphia: Fortress Press, 1987), 192. McFague, who presents several fruitful models of God in this book (Mother, Lover, Friend is the first to echo Thomas Aquinas' "We know God as unknown."

175

30. Dietrich Bonhoeffer, *Letters and Papers from Prison*. The Enlarged Edition. Edited by Eberhard Bethge (London: SCM Press, 1971), 360.
31. Ibid., 282.
32. Ibid.
33. Paul Tillich. *The Shaking of the Foundations* (Baltimore, MD: Penguin Books, 1962 [1949]), 63
34. Gabriel Marcel, *Metaphysical Journal*. Translated by Bernard Wall (Chicago: Henry Regnery, 1952), 163.
35. Helen Keller, *My Life* (Garden City: Doubleday, 1936), 23–24.
36. Dogmatic references to the inner life of the Trinity maintain that the identity of the three persons is a function of being in and of. ". . . .the Father is entirely in the Son and entirely in the Holy Spirit; the Holy Spirit is entirely in the Father and in the Son." Denziger, 704.
37. Thomas Aquinas, *Summa Theologica* I, q. 8, a. 1.
38. Augustine, *Confessions*, Bk. III, Chap. 6, 11.
39. This interpretation of the God's relationship to creation (called panentheism) is an orthodox interpretation as long as the distinction between God and the world is maintained. See Denzinger, 1782.
40. Sallie McFague, *Models of God*, 201.
41. Contemporary theologians phrase the connection more organically as "Grace supposes nature and nature supposes grace." See Richard P. McBrien, *Catholicism*. Revised Edition (New York: Harper SanFrancisco, 1994), 182.
42. Corita Kent in Harvey Cox, *The Feast of Fools*.

CHAPTER 4

1. Dwight D. Eisenhower quoted in Robert N. Bellah, "Civil Religion in America," in Richey and Jones, eds. *American Civil Religion*, 23.
2. See Chapter Two, 54.
3. Wilfred Cantwell Smith, *Faith and Belief* (Princeton: Princeton University Press, 1979), 76.
4. Paul W. Pruyser, *Between Belief and Unbelief* (New York: Harper and Row, 1974), 249–250.
5. Isaiah 7:9 (Septuagint). The thesis is central to Augustine's thought. See *In Joannis Evangelium Tractatus*, xxix, 6; xxvii, 7.
6. Milton Rokeach, *Beliefs Attitudes and Values: A Theory of Organization and Change* (San Francisco: Jossey–Bass, 1969), 3.
7. Pruyser, ibid.

176

8. Ibid.
9. Robert C. Solomon, *The Passions: The Myth and Nature of Human Emotion* (Notre Dame, IN: University of Notre Dame Press, 1983 [1976]), 158–159.
10. A series of experiments in which persons were unknowingly subjected to chemically induced bodily sensations, led the experimenters to these conclusions: Emotions are not physiologically distinguishable. They are labeled according to cues we take from the environment. Physiologically then, love would be the same bodily experience as anger or embarrassment. See S. Schacter and J. E. Singer "Cognitive, Social, and Physiological Determinants of Emotional State," *Psychological Review* 69 (1962), 379–399. While few psychologists hold with these conclusions, Wayne Proudfoot has provocatively grounded his explanation of religious experience in Schacter and Singer's studies. See *Religious Experience* (Berkeley: University of California Press, 1985).
11. Robert C. Solomon, *Love: Emotion, Myth and Metaphor* (Garden City, NY: Doubleday Anchor, 1981), xxviii.
12. Ibid.
13. Silvan S. Thomkins, "Affect as the Primary Motivational System," in *Feelings and Emotions* edited by Magda B. Arnold (New York: Academic Press, 1970), 101–110.
14. John M. Darley and C. Daniel Batson, "'From Jerusalem to Jericho': A Study of Situational and Dispositional Variables in Helping Behavior," *Journal of Personality and Social Psychology* 27:1 (1973), 100–108.
15. Robert O. Johann, *Building the Human* (New York: Herder and Herder, 1968), 145–147.
16. Erik Erikson, *Identity and the Life Cycle*, Psychological Issues 1 (New York: International Universities Press, 1959), 95ff.
17. William James, *Variety*, 164.
18. Holmes, T. H. and Rahe, R. H. "The Social Readjustment Rating Scale," *Journal of Psychosomatic Research.* (1967) 11:213– 218. Reprinted in *Welcome Stress* by William D. Brown. Minneapolis, MN: CompCare Publications, 1983.
19. Walter Conn, *Christian Conversion*, 38.
20. Seymour Epstein, "A Research Paradigm for the Study of Personality and Emotions" in Nebraska Symposium on Motivation 1982, Volume 1 *Personality—Current Theory and Research* (Lincoln: University of Nebraska Press, 1983), 96.
21. Leon Festinger, *A Theory of Cognitive Dissonance* (Stanford, CA: Stanford University Press, 1957), 2.

22. Leon Festinger, Henry W.Riecken and Stanley Schacter *When Prophecy Fails: A Social and Psychological Study of a Modern Group that Predicted the Destruction of the World* (New York: Harper Torchbooks, 1964 [1956]).

23. Robert B. Cialdini, *Influence: How and Why People Agree to Things* (New York: Quill, 1984), 128.

24. David Krathwohl, Benjamin S. Bloom and Bertram Masia, *Taxonomy of Educational Objectives* Handbook II: Affective Domain (New York: David McKay Co., 1964), 33–38.

25. In a wonderful book that traces the story of how people became socially active, Richard A. Hoehn plots a course similar to the one outlined in these pages. Titles of his chapters demonstrate the similarity: "Confrontations," "Coming to Awareness," "Moral Insight," "The Activation of Commitment," "Moral Commitment," and "Moral Conviction." See *Up From Apathy: A Study of Moral Awareness and Social Involvement*. Nashville: Abingdon Press, 1983.

26. Marilyn Ferguson, *The Aquarian Conspiracy* (Boston: Houghton Mifflin, 1980), 337.

27. Berger and Luckmann, *Social Construction of Reality*, 158.

CHAPTER 5

1. Although existentialists differ dramatically on many questions, they share a common conviction that the power to choose distinguishes human beings. We find, for example, Gabriel Marcel using a quote from Nietsche, "Man [sic] is the only being who makes a promise." See Joe McCown, *Availability: Gabriel Marcel and the Phenomenology of Human Openess*, AAR Studies in Religion, 14 (Missoula, MT: Scholars Press, 1978), 69.

2. Margaret A. Farley speaks of interpersonal commitment "as a prime case for understanding all kinds of commitments." *Personal Commitments* (San Francisco: Harper and Row, 1986), 15.

3. Karl Rahner, *The Foundations of Christian Faith* (New York: Seabury, 1978).

4. Jurgen Moltmann, *The Theology of Hope: On the Ground and the Implications of a Christian Eschatology*, trans. James W. Leitch (New York: Harper and Row, 1967), 225, cited in Farley, op. cit., 133.

5. There is general agreement in the Church that everyone is to be in mission, that the mission is "in and to six continents." "Mission and Evangelism: An Ecumenical Affirmation," *Mission Series No. 4*, (Geneva: WCC, 1983), no. 37.

6. John L. McKenzie, "The Gospel According to Matthew," *The Jerome Biblical Commentary*, Raymond E. Brown, Joseph A. Fitzmeyer and Roland E. Murphy, eds. (Englewood Cliffs, NJ: Prentice–Hall, 1968), 113–114.

7. One of these changes is the largely diminished pool of "foreign" missionaries. Even conservative churches are withdrawing these professional missionaries. See Donald A. McGovran, *Momentous Decisions in Mission Today* (Grand Rapids: Baker Book House, 1984), 191 ff.

8. Cited in Luise Ahrens, M.M. Address to Directors of the Society for the Propagation of the Faith. April 22, 1986. New York.

9. Jerald D. Gort, "Christian Historical and Earlier Ecumenical Perceptions," in *Dialogue and Syncretism*, eds. Jerald D. Gort, Hendrik M. Vroom, Rein Fernhout, and Anton Wessels (Grand Rapids: Eerdmans, 1989), 41.

10. Mercy Amba Oduyoye, *Hearing and Knowing: Theological Reflections on Christianity in Africa* (Maryknoll: Orbis, 1986), 33.

11. Robert B. Sheard, *Interreligious Dialogue in the Catholic Church Since Vatican II*, Toronto Studies in Theology, Vol. 31 (Lewiston/Queenston: Edwin Mellon Press, 1987), 24.

12. *Nostra Aetate*, no. 2.

13. Reported by Emilio Castro, "Mission in a Pluralistic Age," *International Review of Mission* LXXV, 299 (July 1986), 200.

14. Willie Jenkinson, CSSp, "Signposts of the Future", *Mission in Dialogue*, Mary Motte, FMM and Joseph R. Lang, MM, eds. (Maryknoll, NY: Orbis, 1982), 660.

15. See the work of Sharon H. Ringe, especially *Jesus, Liberation, and the Biblical Jubilee: Images for Ethics and Christology* (Philadelphia: Fortress Press, 1985).

16. Mary Motte, F.M.M. *A Critical Examination of Mission Today*, Research Project Report, Phase One (Washington, D.C.: United States Catholic Mission Association, 1987), 16–19.

17. One observer at a recent meeting of the World Council of Churches Commission on World Mission and Evangelism in San Antonio, TX described some of the recommendations of the conference as appearing more like those of the United Nations than those of an ecumenical church conference. Norman E. Thomas, "Ecumenical Directions in Mission: Melbourne to San Antonio," *Missiology: An International Review* Vol. XVIII, No. 2 (April, 1990), 155.

18. Mission Vision, Maryknoll Sisters. Proceedings of General Chapter, 1984.

19. *Guidelines on Dialogue* (Geneva: World Council of Churches, 1982), no. 11.

20. John Stott, *"Dialogue, Encounter even Confrontation,"* in *Faith Meets Faith: Mission Trends No. 5*, Gerald H. Anderson and Thomas F. Stransky, eds. (New York: Paulist Press, 1981), 168.

21. Leslie Newbigin, "Religious Pluralism and the Uniqueness of Jesus Christ," *International Bulletin of Missionary Research*, Vol. 13, No. 2 (April, 1989), 54.

22. Paul Knitter, Preface to *The Myth of Christian Uniqueness: Towards a Pluralistic Theology of Religions* John Hick and Paul Knitter, eds. (Maryknoll, NY: Orbis Books, 1987), viii. It is interesting to note this conference also included critics of the position taken in the published papers (John Cobb, Schubert Ogden, David Tracy) who felt that the pluralist move is either "unwarranted, unnecessary or ill-timed." Ibid.

23. Walter Buhlmann, *Courage Church*, trans. Mary Smith (Maryknoll: Orbis, 1978), 82. Gabriel Moran helpfully explores the paradox of uniqueness: "Anything can be conceived in two ways: (A) as a thing that excluded other things in its exclusive possession of space and time; or (B) as a thing that exists only because of the web of relationships that constitute its life." "Is the Holocaust Unique?" *Journal of Ecumenical Studies* Vol. 26, No. 1, 211–216. See also his *Uniqueness*, (Maryknoll, NY: Orbis Books, 1992).

24. Rosemary Radford Ruether, "Feminism and Jewish-Christian Dialogue," in *The Myth of Christian Uniqueness*, 138.

25. Robert B. Sheard, *op. cit.*, 305.

26. "Today, implantation of the church as a primary task of mission has been supplanted largely by other tasks because of the presence of the church in nearly all parts of the world, an experience that opens up new insights [as noted earlier] about what constitutes mission." Mary Motte, F.M.M., *op. cit.*, 17.

27. *Summa Theologica* I–II, q.27, a.1, ad 3.

28. Cited in Gideon Engler, "Aesthetics in Science and Art," *British Journal of Aesthetics*, Vol. 30, No. 1 (January, 1990), 24.

29. *Ibid.*

30. Mary Mothersill, *Beauty Restored* (Oxford: Clarendon Press, 1984).

31. In *The Analogical Imagination* (New York: Crossroad, 1981), David Tracy offers a criterion for good theological use of analogy: "the ability to preserve the tension of the original symbolic language within clarity of the concept." 439. See also *Pluralism and Ambiguity* (San Francisco: Harper and Row, 1987), 20–21.

32. This is an adaptation of Mary Mothersill's descriptions of beauty. She in turn adapts the works of Kant, Aquinas, and Arnold Isenberg in constructing her descriptions.

33. John Dewey, *Logic: The Theory of Inquiry* (New York: Henry Holt, 1938), 128–129.

34. *Ibid.*, 70.

35. Mothersill, *op. cit.*, 324

36. *Ibid.*, 332–335.

37. *Ibid.*, 380.

38. "Mission and Evangelism," No. 10.

39. The Third International Synod of Bishops stated "Action on behalf of justice and participation fully appears to us as *constitutive of the gospel and of the Church's mission* for the redemption of the human race and its liberation from every oppression." *Justice in the World* (Washington: United States Catholic Conference, 1972), 34. Italics mine.

40. Mothersill, *op. cit.*, 167.

41. John F. Haught *What is God* (New York: Paulist, 1986), 71– 82. Haught has a section on God as Beauty. While he does not use the expression "consciousness raising," his suggestions lend themselves to that analogy.

42. Matthew Fox, *A Spirituality Named Compassion and the Healing of the Global Village and Us* (Minneapolis: Winston Press, 1979), vi.

43. Rosabeth Moss Kanter, *Commitment and Community* (Cambridge: Harvard University Press, 1972).

44. Gabriel Marcel, *Creative Fidelity*, trans. Robert Rosthal (New York: Crossroad, 1982 [1940]), 152.

45. Ibid., 154.

46. Farley, *op. cit*, 48–51.

47. See above, Chapter Three, 101.

48. Cited in Farley, 50.

49. Farley, 59.

50. Arthur Koestler, *The Act of Creation* (New York: Macmillan, 1964), 95.

51. Peter Berger, *The Heretical Imperative* (Garden City, NY: Anchor Press/Doubleday, 1979), 18.

52. Selections from Basil, *Longer Rules*, 7, cited in Patrick Gillespie Henry "Monastic Mission," *The Ecumenical Review* 39, 3 (July 1987), 278.

INDEX

❋

A

Aesthetics, 73–75, 77, 81, 82, 150–152, 155
Affect, 116–119
Ahrens, Louise, M.M., 142, 179
Andrade, E.N. da C., 69–70, 173
Apologetics, 13–16
    as Contextualization, 14
Aquinas, Thomas, 103, 106–107, 155, 176, 181
Arendt, Hannah, 75, 174
Aristotle, 53, 69
Augustine, 32, 34–36, 107, 114, 134, 170, 171, 176, 177
Bacon, Francis, 42–43, 55
Barbour, Ian, 44, 59, 171
Beauty, 11, 68, 74, 149–158, 162, 164
Belief, 13, 24, 30, 33, 43, 54, 65, 91, 93, 100, 101, 111–116, 125–129, 131–134, 136,
    The Function of Beliefs, 112

B

Bellah, Robert N., 87, 174, 177
Berger, Peter, 62, 164, 173, 178, 182
Bernstein, Richard J., 54, 172
Birth as Conversion, 100
Blomberg, Craig, 14, 169
Boff, Leonardo, 21, 169
Bohr, Neils, 68–69, 173
Bonhoeffer, Dietrich, 103–105, 176
Borhek, James T., 23, 170
Born, Max, 51, 52, 59, 68, 171
Bronowski, Jacob, 39, 171
Buhlmann, Walter, 148, 181
Butterfield, Herbert, 172

183

C

Certitude, 9–11, 26, 33, 67–70,
72, 74, 84, 85, 87, 103
Chesterton, Gilbert K., 29, 87,
162, 174
Christianity as Counter-Cultural,
25–27
Cialdini, Robert, 129, 178
Cohen, I Bernard, 43, 50, 55, 171
Coll, Regina, 6
Colonization, 45–46
Columbus, 36–37, 53
Commitment, 12, 27, 54, 63–65,
81, 84–85, 118, 135–141,
146, 149, 153;
elements of, 136;
meaning of, 137;
to God, 139–142;
nurturing, 159–165
Conflict, 27, 88, 91, 95, 101, 109,
111, 112, 120, 124–126, 128,
130–132, 134, 135;
nature of, 126–128
Conn, Walter E., 88, 90, 91, 99,
126, 175, 178
Contemplation, 27, 96, 97, 111,
120, 124
Context and Existence, 18
Contextualization, 14, 15, 23
Conversion, 12, 27, 53–54,
87–94, 96–104, 107–109,
111, 112, 115, 116, 120, 122,
125, 126, 130–134, 142, 146,
159, 161, 165; kinds of 88–91
Conviction, 9, 26, 30, 43, 47, 84,
85, 87, 93, 95, 96, 123, 128,
132, 135, 143, 157, 166
Copernicus, 39–40, 43, 48, 49, 53
Coughlin, Ellen K., 52, 171
Coulson, John, 25, 170
Council of Jerusalem, 16

Cox, Harvey, 12, 108, 110, 177
Criteria, 27, 52, 57, 72, 73, 77,
78, 81, 82, 84, 111, 134, 153
Curtis, Richard F., 24, 170

D

Darwin, Charles, 42, 43, 45
Definition, 17, 22, 65, 83, 115,
158
Demetrakopoulos, Stephanie,
100, 176
Dewey, John, 73, 74, 77, 78, 155,
156, 173, 174, 181
Dialogue, 147–149
Dirac, Paul, 151
Discernment, 68, 124
Dispassion, 54, 55, 87
Drake, Stillman, 40, 69, 171, 173
Durka, Gloria, 6, 49
Dying as Conversion, 99

E

Ecumenical movement, 10, 142
Einstein, Albert, 23, 42, 48–49,
55
Eisenhower, Dwight D., 111, 177
Eliade, Mircea, 32, 170
Engler, Gideon, 151
Enlightenment, 24, 26, 27, 44, 46,
85
Epistemology, 31, 46
Epstein, Seymour, 126, 178
Erikson, Erik, 125, 178
Eucharist, 158, 165
Evangelizing, 18–19, 28, 149–159
Existentialism, 48, 179
Experience, 26, 31, 35, 37, 38,
40, 41, 43–46, 49–51, 58–61,

63–65, 70, 72–74, 77–81, 85,
88, 92–94, 96, 98–100, 108,
112–119, 123–127, 130–132,
139, 144, 149, 152, 155, 155,
158, 159, 161, 162

F

Farley, Margaret A., 138, 141,
160–162, 179, 182
Ferguson, Marilyn, 133
Festinger, Leon, 128, 129
Fowler, James W., 89–91, 174,
175
Fox, Matthew, 159, 182
Fragoso Nevarez, Maria del
Socorro, 6

G

Galileo, 36, 39–40, 43, 53, 69
Glock, Charles, 31, 170
God as Sheer In-ness and Of-ness,
103–107
God's Role in Conversion,
101–103
Gort, Jerald D., 142, 179
Grace, 12, 108–109, 145,
158–160, 162
Grof, Stanislav, 100, 176

H

Hanson, Norwood, 53, 172
Hart, Ray L., 58, 172
Harris, Maria, 6, 96–97, 101, 175
Haught, John F., 182
Haughton, Rosemary, 97–98, 175
Heisenberg, Werner, 50

Henry, Patrick, 6, 165, 182
Hick, John, 172–173, 174
Hoehn, Richard A., 178

I

Imagination, 25, 27, 41, 47, 49,
54, 55, 57–60, 65, 73, 76, 77,
94–96, 117, 152
Impressionism, 45
Incarnation, 19, 26, 140–141, 158
Inculturation, 21–23, 26
Indigenization, 23
Individual's Contribution to the
Netting of Reality, 63–65

J

James, William, 29, 35, 59, 77,
91–92, 95, 96, 101, 125, 170,
172, 178
Jenkinson, Willie CSSp, 145, 180
"Jerusalem to Jericho"
Experiment, 120–121, 178
Jesus, 10, 15, 19, 26, 37, 83, 140,
144–148, 159, 165
Jesus Seminar, 10
Johann, Robert O., 122, 178
Justice, 35, 93, 138, 146, 158,
159, 181–182

K

Kanter, Rosabeth Moss, 160
Keller, Helen, 105–106, 176
Kent, Corita, 12, 109, 169, 177
Knitter, Paul, 148, 180
Knowing as Conversion, 94–95
Knowledge, 24, 26–27, 30–35,

41–45, 50, 52, 54, 55, 57–59,
  62, 64, 65, 67, 68, 70, 72, 73,
  79, 82, 95, 102–104, 112,
  154, 164
Knowledge as Experience, 41–46
Knowledge as Revelation, 31–35
Koestler, Arthur, 163, 182
Kubler Ross, Elisabeth, 99, 175
Kuhn, Thomas S., 51–54, 62, 66,
  171–172, 173

L

Langer, Suzanne, 73, 173
Language, 15, 18–21, 25, 39, 48,
  59, 61, 62, 68, 80, 98, 101,
  106, 117, 142, 149, 151, 152,
  155, 157,
  Vernacular, 19, 20
Laplace, Pierre de, 44, 45, 103
Littlewood, Joan, 46
Loder, James F., 94, 95, 101, 175
Love as Conversion, 97
Luckmann, Thomas, 62, 173, 178
Lycurgus, 32

M

Marcel, Gabriel, 105, 135, 161,
  176, 178, 182
Marshal, I Howard, 25, 170
Masterman, Margaret, 54, 172
McDermott, John, 35
McFague, Sallie, 103, 107, 176
McBrien, Richard P., 176
McGovran, Donald A., 179
McKenzie, John L., 141, 179
McLean, Stuart D., 89, 174
Meaning, 13, 17, 21, 36, 61, 62,
  67, 68, 70, 71, 75, 78, 82,

83, 115, 136, 137, 159, 162,
  166
Missionaries, 11, 141–147, 179
Moltmann, Jurgen, 141, 179
Moran, Gabriel, 181
Moses, 31–32, 40
Motte, Mary, F.M.M., 26, 145,
  146, 149, 180, 181
Mothersill, Mary, 152, 155–157,
  181–182

N

Newbigin, Leslie, 148–149, 180
Newton, Isaac, 42, 43, 45, 49, 53
Nida, Eugene A., 20
Nostra Aetate, 143–144, 180
Nurturing Commitment, 159

O

O'Gorman, Edmundo, 36–38,
  170, 171
O'Rourke, David K., 88, 174
Ornstein, Robert, 65, 173
Oduyoye, 142–143, 179
Osei-Bonsu, Joseph, 20–21, 169
Our Role in Conversions, 108

P

Paradigm, 15, 52–54, 66, 93, 126
Pasquier, 99, 176
Pattern of conversion, 27, 101
Pelikan, Jaroslav, 83, 174
Physics, 43, 46, 48–51, 54, 62, 68,
  70, 78, 173
Plato, 32–34

Pluralism, 29, 46, 51, 54, 55, 59,
   81, 82, 85, 104, 148, 152, 159,
   Temptations of, 54–56
Polanyi, Michael, 172
Positivism, 44
Pruyser, Paul, 113–115, 177
Puzo, Mario, 91, 175

R

Rahner, Karl, 141, 179
Rambo, Lew, 93, 175
Reality, defining, 58;
   flavoring, 60
Relating, 161, 164–165
Relativism, 27, 54, 55, 57, 65, 70,
   74, 81, 84, 111, 153
Relaxing, 161–162, 165
Religion as a Private Affair, 24–25
Religious Traditions, an analogy,
   152–155
Remembering, 161, 162
Revelation, 19, 26, 30–32, 35–36,
   39, 44, 72, 140, 162
Ringe, Sharon, 145, 180
Roddick, Nick, 171
Rokeach, Milton, 114, 177
Role of Society in Netting Reality,
   61–63
Romantic Movement, 44
Ross, James, 35, 99, 101, 170
Roulet, Elaine, 6
Roulet, Jean M., 6
Ruether, Rosemary Radford, 149,
   174, 181
Rush, Molly, 93, 175

S

Sartre, Jean Paul, 48
Schacter and Singer Experiments,
   177

Schreiter, Robert J., 26, 170
Schuh, Dolores, 6
Sheard, Robert B., 143, 149, 180,
   181
Smith, Suzanne, 6
Smith, John, 88, 174
Smith, Suzanne, 6
Smith, W. Cantwell, 83, 113,
   174, 177
"Social Readjustment Rating
   Scale", 125–126
Solomon, Robert C., 117–119,
   177
Stott, John, 147, 180
Substance and accident, 22
Subverting the Era of Experience,
   46
Subverting the Era of Revelation,
   35

T

Taxonomy of Affect, 131–134,
   178
Teaching, 18–19, 76, 94–96,
   130–132, 141, 143
Teaching as Conversion, 96
Theater of the Absurd, 48
Thomkins, Silvan S., 119, 177
Thompson, Norma, 49, 171
Tillich, Paul, 105, 176
Tolerance, 24, 55, 82, 87
Tracy, David, 152, 181
Transformation, 27, 90, 98, 132,
   134, 138, 139, 141
Translation, 18–21, 149
   Difficulties of, 20–21
Trinity, 106, 176
Truth, 27, 34, 35, 46, 55, 56, 58,
   62, 65–67, 70–72, 74, 129,
   144, 147–151;
   Models of, 66–71

V

Vespucci, Amerigo, 36–38

W

Waldseemuller, Martin, 38
Whitehead, Alfred North, 32, 170
World Council of Churches, 142,
     144, 147, 180
World War I, 46–48
Worldview, 29, 30, 48

Y

Yeats, William Butler, 47, 171
Young, Josiah U., 23, 125, 170